SHINE!

VOLUME II

*Inspirational Stories of Choosing
Success Over Adversity*

PROMINENCE PUBLISHING

Published by Prominence Publishing.

For information visit www.prominencepublishing.com

Cover design by Prominence Publishing.

ISBN: 978-1-988925-06-6

First Edition: September 2017

CONTENTS

Introduction

I am a big believer in creating a life that you love. I work hard to surround myself with positive, successful people. To that extent, I am careful about the projects I choose and the authors I choose to work with.

I feel incredibly honoured to be a part of this project. The co-authors of this book are amazing! As you read their stories that follow, you may start to feel like you're getting to know these women. That's my intention. I want you to curl up with a cup of tea and really *feel* these stories. I want you to know that you are not alone. Although many of the co-authors of this book have had to overcome seemingly insurmountable challenges, they persevered, they fought, and they won. And they're here to tell you that you can do it, too.

Our first volume of SHINE was published only 4 short months ago. Right after that book was launched, it became a massive success and was named a best seller and a Hot New Release on Amazon in 9 different categories! What really touched me was the number of women who reached out to me, saying, "Thank you. Because of that book and because of those women sharing their stories, I know that I can do it too."

I recently realized that I don't just help people write books and get published. I help people **believe** that they can. Every person on the planet has a gift and that gift needs to be shared with the world. I help people realize that gift and get it out to the world in the form of books. And I feel so lucky to be able to do that!

We all face challenges and times of adversity. It's how you choose to respond that matters. You can choose to succeed in times of adversity. You can choose to win. You always have a choice. You are never alone. If you need help, reach out to someone. If they can't help you or they don't understand, try someone else. You are never alone. You can do this!

To your success,

Suzanne Doyle-Ingram

Publisher
Prominence Publishing

You Become Strong When it is the Only Choice That You Have

By Sheri Scott

S pringhouse Architects is a strong business. We are serving clients and growing every year. I started the business by myself in 2008. It was a bit of a rough start but has been a great climb ever since.

Many architects I know have some romantic story about when they were ten years old and had a calling to architecture. Not me. When I was in high school, I had a rough time. I was making bad choices and hanging with the wrong crowds. My parents had divorced recently, and both of my siblings had left for college, and I was kind of lost. Although he doesn't admit it, my dad, who I was living with at the time, called the high school and told them, "Get Sheri to pick something. Get her to apply to colleges and go do something." The counselor called me down to her office and asked me what my plans, dreams and goals were? I replied (in my best seventeen-year-old annoyed voice), "I don't know what I want to do and I really don't care." She said, "How about engineering?" because my dad is an engineer, my sister is an engineer, my uncle is an engineer, and I said, "Anything but an engineer." So she offered, "How about an architect?" and I said, "Fine. Sign me up." That was all of the thought that went into that decision. It is true that teachers and counselors have a huge impact on kids. That flippant decision turned out to be exactly the right choice for me. I am forever grateful to that counselor.

I was accepted into The University of Cincinnati, Design, Architecture, Art and Planning (DAAP) college. Well, as a probationary student. My grades were not great toward the end of high school but I tested well and I believe the college was looking to bolster their female numbers in architecture. I was intrigued to enter a male dominated field. I saw it as a challenge and something that would be special. DAAP was a top ten college of architecture in the country, and I was excited to have that opportunity. One of the best advantages I got out of college was the co-op experience. Starting in second year, we alternated 3 months of school with 3 months of work. Co-oping allowed me to try different avenues within architecture. I thought going into school that I would work at a huge architecture firm and climb the corporate ladder; however, my path couldn't have been more different. I learned what I wanted to do and where I wanted to be because of my co-oping opportunities during college. Once I graduated, I was focused and ready.

Focused and ready, except I had been dating this guy, John. We met right as I graduated high school, dated long distance all through college and married in my final year. John is 6 years older than me, and it took seven years to complete my bachelors of architecture. We started a family right away, so when I was searching for my first job I had to make specific decisions directly related to being a female architect and mother. I tried to come from a position of power and make a decision of where I wanted to be, the kind of job I wanted, and what my schedule would be. That was a difficult approach. Every person I interviewed with was a middle aged white man. I presented my philosophy of how I wanted to live an integrated life with work and home and how that was the best way for me to offer them my very best work. Their reactions were mixed. I ended my search when I found Atelier Design. They were the same demographic as all the others, but they took the time to discuss an approach that would be mutually beneficial. Our arrangement for most of the twelve years I was there was basically less money for more flexibility. It worked for me. It worked for them. I was proud of the work I did there. You don't have to fit into a mold to contribute. Sometimes you need to forge your own path to get where you are supposed to go.

I spent twelve years at Atelier Design working hard for them designing custom homes, but there came a time when I was ready for a change. Ready for more of a challenge. Our three boys were in school full time. While Atelier was a great job for me, it was what many people call a 'place holder' job. A job where a mother can work hard, learn, and keep her foot in the door while the rest of her body and heart are busy raising a family. I was considering going out on my own.

There is one specific day that I can remember so vividly from this time. It was the middle of the morning. I was on my regular scheduled day off work. The boys were all at school. I was sitting at the kitchen table working on a business plan to launch my own architecture firm. I heard the garage door go up and John walked in the house. He asked me what I was working on. I told him, and he replied, "We might need to rethink that, I was just asked to resign from my job." *What? John lost his job. What does that mean?* He was the bread winner of the family. He set our routine for the day. He was a prosecuting attorney and he identified his worth with his job.

We quickly decided that John would find another job as a prosecuting attorney because that is what he did. He did receive an offer of employment very quickly. It basically replaced his salary and benefits but we had to move to another state. We thought we were so lucky. How fortunate that we can just continue on like nothing happened. It will all be exactly the same. Parents and friends encouraged us to slow down and take a breath. But we knew...we were sure... So many decisions moved so fast from that moment. I will recount them as I remember but details are light because it was all a blur.

John took the job.

I stayed to get the boys through the end of the school year.

I had surgery on both legs from a running injury.

We put the house up for sale.

I quit my job.

I filed the papers to start my own architecture business.

We bought a house in Indiana.

John's new job seemed fine.

We moved.

Boys started school.

We sold the old house.

I made friends.

The boys made friends.

We were settling in.

John's mom was diagnosed with cancer.

His mom died.

Funeral.

John asked to take on a more significant role at work.

The boys were active with sports and friends.

John's job was switched due to office politics.

The job wasn't good.

John's dad was diagnosed with cancer.

John had a complete mental break.

All in three months.

One day was like all the others. Three boys up, fed and off to school. I started work in my home office. John wasn't coming downstairs to head to his downtown office. I thought *That's weird, but he has been quiet lately.* After about an hour I went up to check on him. He wasn't in the bedroom. He wasn't in the bathroom or any of the boys' rooms. That's when I went into our walk in closet and found my strong, proud husband curled up on the floor crying. And then not crying, which was actually worse. He couldn't tell me what was wrong. It was nothing, and it was everything.

I was scared for him. I remember texting my sister and asking her to call me, "It's important, I think I need to take John to the hospital." She called right away, and we talked through the options. What do you do when a person is unresponsive but not hurt in any physical way? Then, because of the attitudes and judgements of mental illness you also have to weigh who will find out, what will it affect adversely, will someone make a decision against our will? Who can help? What can they do?

I thank God to this day that I did not find him dead from suicide. That is how lost he felt, but he held on to some sliver of strength to not do that.

The depression and mental break was not mine, but it quickly became my issue. As a wife, mother and business owner I was busy. I had my head down doing what needed to be done. With so many life transitions happening all in that span of three months I didn't look up. At the time I had no perspective of my husband's mounting pressures. I didn't see the decline he was going through. I'm not sure I could have prevented it, but I am sure I could have been better prepared and possibly have lessened the blow we all took.

In the first two weeks, I was scared for John. Then I was scared for me. Every routine thing about my life changed in that one day. We were a contemporary couple. We both worked, we did chores and raised our boys together. All of a sudden it was just me. John's recovery would take months of rest, quiet and family support. He wasn't able to drive, he couldn't focus long enough to pay the bills, and at the beginning of his recovery, he basically couldn't participate in life.

They say you don't decide to become strong. You become strong when it is the only choice you have. Well, in a new town with three young boys, keeping my new business going, and nursing my husband back to health - it quickly became the only choice I had. Appointments, bills, meds, insurance coverage, family medical leave, taking the trash out, homework, practices, family time, birthdays, suicide watch, oil changes, working, sleeping, eating.

It was exhausting, but I could do it. We had many people supporting us. My sister checked on me every day. My mother visited, and I remember feeling incredibly grateful that she talked to John like he was normal and this was a thing we were going to work through. My dad visited and shared stories with us of people he knew that went through similar trials. New friends in our community reached out with a genuineness that I've never experienced before. My aunt Barb called and told me, "Go ahead and cry, honey." I did. I sobbed. God, it was so hard. The emotional energy it took to hold it all together was incredible.

With rest, medication and therapy, John began to recover. It was literally a brain injury. Stress is a killer. Hormones and chemical reactions to stress flood the brain. Our bodies are amazing at how much we can resist, but eventually, it is too much. It takes time for the brain to recover. After the first two months, he went back to work for a short time, quickly to discover that this was no longer what he wanted to do. Although he had been on family leave, we decided together that he needed a change. By some special grace and good old fashioned hard work, my business was growing. However, it was growing back in Dayton, Ohio, where we had moved from. Dayton is where all of my architecture connections and clients were. We made the difficult decision to move back.

We waited until the boys finished their current term in school and it was Christmas break. With John quitting work, my new business growing but still fledgling, and looking to sell another house in a down market, we needed some help. We were blessed to accept a loan from my father, and he offered for us to move into his Dayton home until we could get our feet under us again. Yet another blow to a proud couple that really just wants everything to get back to normal.

We made the move. Eventually, we bought our own house. John started his own attorney practice but never really settled into that as a job. After a couple of years, he accepted a new position as an assistant prosecuting attorney. This was three years after the mental break and it was the first time I believed things were headed back to normal. Our new normal, of course. John is back. He is a strong attorney and an excellent prosecutor.

I continued building my business. Now in our tenth year, we are still moving forward. I have a total of 7 team members that work hard and serve clients. I am proud to have created a company that offers flexibility at work. All of our employees are remote. They work from their own homes and offices. We have a commitment to work really hard and produce really good things. If we can all do that, then we can be flexible about schedules and let you design your own best life. When I was searching for my first job I was looking for flexibility because I was a new mother. I have come to find that flexibility is a personal issue, not a female issue. Our approach has been successful and success is the best way to effect change.

This experience has changed me. It changed us all forever. If anyone were to ask my advice for surviving a trial like this, I have a few things to offer.

- Keep your head up. Not after the fact, but before. Be aware of what others are going through and how they are reacting to it.

- Find mature people. I had no idea that mental illness affects so many people. One way I was helped the most was mature people in my life talking to me about experiences they have had or known. It makes you feel normal.

- Accept help. Most people don't know what to do or say but when they offer to take a kid to practice or to make a dinner - just let them.

- Talk about it. It is still difficult for me to talk about this time in our lives. Not only because the shame of mental illness still holds but because it is emotional and difficult to recount. I'm telling this story because it is a story my boys need to know. It is a story that we need to not be ashamed of. It is a story of family and strength and growth that we can be proud of.

- Lastly, help others. I have grown much stronger and much more independent through this experience. "Be the person you needed at the hardest time in your life" is a mantra I try to live by. While I have not had the opportunity to help someone through mental illness, I have been able to draw on my difficulty in high school. I believe that the way I can empower, teach and lift up women is to mentor teen girls. When my world was falling apart at 16 years old, what I wouldn't have given to have one person check in on me, ask me how I was doing, or tell me they were thinking of me. Because of that experience, I now mentor four teenage girls. They are each unique and came to me organically just doing life together. I believe that we connect in this life by being open to the opportunity to be there for someone else.

This story is complicated for us. Many of our friends still don't know what we went through. The shame and misunderstanding of mental health keep us from telling our story and it keeps our dear friends from asking. Gender stereotypes also play a part on keeping silent. For John being a man it is unacceptable to need a break. As an attorney it is even more taboo to ask for help and therefore it is the profession with the one of the highest alcohol addiction and suicide rates. The American Bar Association has two groups specifically dedicated to helping but it seems they are making slow progress.

It is also complicated for a woman in a male dominated profession to show vulnerability. My life has been a constant study in integration of all parts of my life. I have drinks with girlfriends at 3pm. I have evening meetings. I take off a full morning to volunteer at the high school. I also work at night on the couch while my family watches tv. It is simply life. All of it. Until we can integrate all the joy and complications without segmenting out work, we won't get anywhere. It is a question of being authentic.

This all happened to John, but it happened to me too. In a different way. In a more helpless, ineffective, terrifying way. All while I was faking my way through being a strong, independent business builder. It made me stronger as a person, and it made us stronger as a family.

About the Author, Sheri Scott

Website: www.SpringhouseArchitects.com
email: sheri@springhousearchitects.com
LinkedIn: linkedin.com/in/sheri-scott
Facebook: facebook.com/springhousearchitects/
Twitter: @SpringhouseArch
Instagram: sheridscott

At my firm, Springhouse Architects, we guide our clients through the entire custom home process. Our clients have worked very hard to get where they are. They are looking for the perfect house that meets their needs and their dreams. The perfect house for their family whether they are a couple just starting out, an active family full of kids and parents and friends, or the empty nesters ready to make a shift.

Unfortunately, the perfect house isn't always waiting for them. Most of our clients don't choose to take on a custom home project as their first choice. It creates great demands on your time, your patience, and it is expensive. Many times, in the backs of their minds they are wondering: Will this be too hard? Will it complicate my marriage? Will we make costly mistakes? The homeowners that do decide to work with us have decided - We have worked so hard, we deserve this. And, your home is where your life happens, it should support your best life.

At Springhouse Architects, we understand you have never done this before. It can be intimidating, and you want to get it right. Through over 20 years of practice in residential architecture, I have seen all of the pitfalls. You can see from our portfolio of over 200 projects and testimonials from clients throughout the years that we know how to guide you through this entire process so that you end up with a great house and you can actually enjoy this exciting process. In fact, I have written a book answering the most common questions I get when new clients start this process. "Dream. Inspire. Design. What a Residential Architect Wants to Tell You About the Custom Home Process." You can download it for free from our website or buy a hard copy from Amazon.com.

Our process is simple.

First, we LISTEN. We listen to you to understand your life, your family, and your dreams. Our clients bring in a ton of inspiration. Finding out what you like and why you like it, how it will serve your family, and helping you decide what fits in your budget is our very first step. You bring everything to us including your style and your ideas; we help you sort through it all.

Then we PLAN. We design your home pulling together all of the information you bring to us, adding in our expertise and design innovation. Through a series of design sessions and meetings, one step at a time, we develop a plan for your home together. You end up with your perfect house for you because you are involved at each step.

Finally, we BUILD. We advocate for you through the entire building process so you can hit your goals, budget, and timelines. During construction is when many of the pitfalls happen. We work with you to ensure all of the work we have done together gets translated exactly as we imagined it.

If you or anyone you know is considering building a custom home, call us, let's talk about your project and see if we can guide you through one of the most exciting, fulfilling, once in a lifetime experiences. You will end up with the perfect house for your family.

Even When You Think You Can't, You Can!

By Alicia Hill-Marceau

Head hung low, body hunched over, eyes only looking at my feet beneath me, breath shallow and waiting to have the permission to exhale, heart physically aching for the approval of others and shame leading the pack. This was my everyday life when I was out in the world and not in the comfort of my own four walls. There, I was protected from the stares of disgust. There, I could eat without the shame. There, I could be this circus creature and not have to worry who I was offending. In my four walls, I felt safe, even though I didn't feel safe or protected in my own skin.

You are probably wondering what physical abnormality it was that I had that would cause this much repulsiveness from the outside world. Did I have my organs baring on the outside of my body? Did I have one too many facial features? An extra nose maybe or an ear on my forehead? What could be so grotesque to the world and the people that assume they are perfect enough to judge others? Here it is...I was fat. That's right. F.A.T. I weighed over 300 pounds. I am short and carried all my weight in my face and stomach. The thing that was harder to carry than the weight itself was the shame. It pushed me so far into the ground I felt as though I would never rise above this feeling. It wasn't just the shame that was lassoed onto me by others; it was my own shame of unworthiness. It was the shame of not being who I knew I was meant to be. It was the shame all of my bad choices compiling together to create a 300-pound monstrosity. I was ashamed of what I looked like but not who I was. If you were to ask others, they would say that I was fun loving and caring with a sense of humor. I was kind to everyone I met including those I knew wanted nothing to do with me. My heart and soul would be described physically as a super model on the runway, but my body would be described as the sludge lying at the bottom of the swamp. Now if only I could get these two to meet and make an average, confident woman. Here is how I did just that by choosing success over my adversity.

I decided that it was time I chose to make a change in my life. I was so tired emotionally and physically of this shame that I carried around with me. And this extra weight that I was lugging around with me was getting to become too much for me to bear. The question was now that I have decided to make this change, how do I go about it? For me, it was something I spent a few years thinking about – weight loss surgery. I knew that this would be the route that I needed to take in order for me to succeed.

I called my family doctor to get a referral to the specialist that would be performing my surgery. I would like to clarify that I thought that this was the solution to all of my problems. Once I had surgery somehow my life would become magically perfect. That was completely false. I would soon learn that this surgery was only one of the tools in my toolbox toward a new healthy life and the rest of them were up to me to decide what they were and how I needed to use them to my own advantage. I had to learn what would help me and what would hinder me. I knew right away that I needed to get my mind right. I had to begin to practice having a thin mind before I got the thin body that I was longing for. I started watching the people around me, not just the super thin but the average person and how they reacted in certain situations like when food was present. Did they have their food detecting radars on when food was around or was it just a part of the scenery? To a fat person if food is around you are either ignoring it like a year old parking ticket, or you are elbow deep in the 7 layer dip. I had to find my place, a new place. I had to learn that food was only a minuscule part of my everyday life. I needed to take away the power I had given to it. I needed to take my power back. My kryptonite was food and not the healthy food that fueled your body in a good way but instead the food that would drive your blood sugar up and make you lethargic. The food that made you want to have a nap instead of running a marathon. My power was knowing that this way that I feel was being affected by the poor choices I was making. My power was learning how I could change that. I needed a new road map to health. Not this map that was slowing guiding me to an early grave. I had to create my own map by changing how I would get to this new destination. I had to avoid the craters and potholes that were taking me to a bad hollow place and follow the new elevated route to a destiny I could never have imagined for myself.

Once all of the facts were staring at me in black and white, and new solutions were being replaced with the old problems, it was time to mentally prepare. I had to get rid of all these dust bunnies that were crowding my attic and replace them with these new fluttering beams of positivity and light. I had to dig deep into my attic (or the addict in me) and figure out how I got to where I was both physically and mentally. This part was harder than the surgery itself. It is scary when we go back to our past and feel the pain all over again. We are opening a wound that we never thought would heal. It has to be done in order to move through it and move forward.

As I remained in this world of obesity, I felt as though as I was all alone. But I wasn't, my family was waiting for me on the outside, reaching for me, yearning for me. Instead of letting them in, I would come up with any and all excuses as to why I couldn't or can't. Every time I said no there really was no good excuse as to why I couldn't besides pure laziness and selfishness. I would rather be alone and lazy than with my children. I could say that it was because I was overweight. I could say that it was because I felt as though I could not move as gracefully as I used to or I could tell the truth. And that is that my stuff was more important than my children. This was a lie that I told myself. It wasn't how I truly felt; it was how my emotions, my shame, my hatred made me feel. And in turn made me believe how I felt about my own children.

More than anything I wanted to be that Mom that I knew I was deep down. The Mom that would run and play with my children and feed them vegetables because they actually liked them not because it was a punishment. Every time I said no or made an excuse not to, I would emotionally punish myself later. *"Alicia, how could you turn them down again? They need you. You are such a crappy Mom to be putting your addiction to food first. You are so lazy. Why is your husband staying with you? Your kids deserve better than you as their Mom. You SUCK, now go and eat something that you think is going to make you feel better and take all this pain away."* This is what I would tell myself every time I felt as though I was sucking at Motherhood, wifehood or even just life in general. I would try and numb the pain away with shame. If I was mean enough to myself, it would hurt less than knowing the pain that I was causing to my own children and my husband. It would become a vicious cycle and my husband, children and myself would continue to suffer if I didn't make a change. They deserved better. I deserved better.

Deciding to have surgery was not a flippant idea that I came up with on a whim. I put a lot of thought into it. I read four books on the surgery itself. I spent almost a year and a half with my surgeon doing all the pre-surgery stuff. I saw an internal medicine specialist, a sleep therapist, a counsellor (my choice, not required), and most importantly I sought out people who themselves had the surgery, either online through forums or in person. I was lucky enough to sit down with someone that allowed me to bombard her with question after question. She was more than willing to answer everything that I needed answered. This was the process that I needed for me to know that what I was doing was the right thing for my future and the success that I was yearning for. Having a surgeon that gave me the tough love that I needed through his words and actions and also remaining very encouraging when I showed him that I would do the work was very helpful in my journey. He sat on the side of my bed moments before the surgery and reassured me that he would take care of me made me feel that I could leave it all in his capable hands.

I was and still am very grateful for him and how devoted he is to his patients.

I spent a few months with a therapist who helped guide me through my pain and prepare me for my new lifestyle and my new mindset that came with it. I learned how to change my language and my thoughts. I learned how to let go of my past and focus on the future I wanted and needed for myself. I was becoming a new me, and I hadn't even had my weight loss surgery yet. But I was ready. It was my time.

Now that fun part begins: after all the hard work I get to see the results happening. The first thing that I noticed was my change in appetite. I used to crave sugar, and now all I want is protein. My clothes were quickly becoming very loose on me. Cleaning out my closet was becoming my new favorite thing to do. My body was able to do things physically that I was not able to do before such as run up and down the stairs with ease, walk for long periods of time, enjoying the scenery and conversation and not watching my clock wondering when the torture would be over. Best of all was being able to cross my legs with ease. I had wanted to do this for many, many years and now I can. My confidence was soaring, and my happiness was palpable, and boy did I love my new life.

Enjoying my new life had really awakened something transformational inside me, and I knew that I needed to share my story. I would walk down the street, and I could see on so many people's faces that pain that I once wore. The pain that said *I am not enough*. The pain that ached in our hearts wanting to be released. They needed to know that life could be better. They needed to know that they didn't have to live in their pain and shame forever. I wanted to help them. But how? I needed to share my story; I needed to write about my journey. And I did. I opened up my soul, and I dug as deep as I could into all my own pain so that I could help others to understand that they are not alone. If someone just like them can come free from the pain that shackled them to their past, then so could they. I titled my book Finally Me because that is how I felt in my life now that I have finally become myself.

I want this feeling for everyone, especially those that have felt lost. You can be yourself again. I was on such a high physically from the weight loss and emotionally from the shame loss. I did not want people to assume that I was selling surgery as an answer but what I was sharing was that once you truly decide to do all the work on all levels that you could choose success over any and all adversities. It is not a quick fix, and it never will be. It is a continuous work of art and even when you think that you have it all figured out life will throw you a curve ball. It is about ADJUSTING AND POSITIVITY.

Adjusting the paths to continue to succeed if our old paths are no longer working for us. An example, once I had lost 132 pounds and was feeling great, wrote my book, the highs of my success began to feel like they were over. I had reached the top, and the only thing left to do was plummet. WRONG. Once you have gone as far as you can, that is when you dig deeper and climb even higher. That is when you adjust your route to get to the highest of peaks. You continue to do this every single time you feel as though you cannot go any further. This is where you will find your strength. In those moments of feeling like we have gone as far or as high as we can, this is when we find in ourselves the strength to carry on higher and higher. Having continual goals is great for your confidence, your success and your soul.

Positivity is an attitude that will get things done with a smile on your face. It will help get you anywhere a heck of a lot quicker than a negative one will. An example is when I had reached my rock bottom before I had had my surgery. I realized that the next step I took would either change my life for the better or the worse. I was over 300 pounds, I was miserable and was at my lowest. I describe this feeling as if I were a balloon blown up to its capacity and I only had two choices. I could choose the negative and burst, which could mean death or I could be positive and deflate, choosing a better life for myself. I decided to deflate, and I did that in more ways than just the weight loss. As I was deflating, losing weight, I was also releasing all the shame, fear, self-hatred, disgust and so much more. After all my air was finally released was when I chose that what would only come into my body from now on was things that served me in a positive way, such as self-love, excitement, kindness, joy and patience. This has done wonders for me because every time something doesn't go my way, I remind myself this could be for a reason, remain positive and it will all work out for the best. And more often than not, it always works out. It may not be what I thought or wanted, but in the long run, it is always best for what is needed in my life at the time.

Fast forward two and a half years, and I am one year out of surgery. I have done all of the work, both emotionally and physically and I have lost 132 pounds. I am feeling FANTASTIC. I finally have my soul and my body on the same page, and I have become the confident average woman that I want to be. I am not a super model by any means, but I am the woman, the Alicia, I always knew I had inside of me. I am happy, confident and I feel beautiful. It was and never will be just because of the weight loss or the surgery. It is because I chose to give myself a better life. It is because I took my power back from food and from strangers who I gave it to because of my own shame. It is because I put myself first now by taking care of my body, my heart and my mind.

If you were to see me walk in public now, you would see a woman who holds her head and her body up high. A woman who takes pride in how she looks. A woman who takes the time to talk and smile with strangers. A woman who looks you in the eyes and no longer at her feet below her. You will see me coming because my confidence and smile enter the room first and my body shows up second.

Five Tips to Choosing Success Over Adversity

1. Take the time needed to figure out first what your adversity/problem is and what the success that you want looks like. What is the problem that you are having and what

do you need to do to find a solution and work towards your success? Remember success is never given. It is earned with hard work and determination. For me, I had to spend time looking at the life that I had and decide what the life I wanted looked like.

2.   Choose to make a change. Now that you know there is a problem or adversity, you want a change or a solution. You choose. Every day you need to choose, and for some, every moment it is a choice: the life you want over the life you have. The CHOICE is yours.

3.   Time to take your POWER back. This is one of the most important steps because you could know what you want, you could choose what you want, but if the adversity, the problem, still holds the power, you will never succeed. You need to hold your own power. You need to be in the driver's seat. You need the control so you can decide your destination.

4.   Here comes the hard part...DO THE WORK. We cannot have a wish and a dream and expect change to come to us without putting the hard work in. This step is never ending. You have to constantly and consistently do the work necessary to your change. For me, it continues to be writing. This helps me to know what is going on for me and what changes need to be made. What is working that I can keep the same? The writing is my guideline to the success that I want and the continued success that I strive for. I have also found that my writing, be it on my blogs or the book I have written (Finally Me, thanks to Vertical Sleeve Gastrectomy) are helping others because I am relatable. If I can do it then so can you. Your WORK could be something different. Figure out what that is for you and DO YOUR WORK!

5.   And lastly and most importantly: POSITIVITY. A good mindset is the key to your success. You can have all the other tips/tools but if you don't think you can, you never will. One of your biggest powers with choice, knowledge, work etc. is being and always remaining positive. Think of positivity as

you breathe, if you want to live you need to breathe. If you want success (life), you need positivity (breathe). You can have one without the other, but your success will never be lifelong. A person who is positive knows that even if your destination has changed or we face a road block, it will always work out. We just know that. Keep positive and stay positive and success is close behind.

I will honestly say that not everything is easy or perfect now because it was never supposed to be. How are we able to learn and grow if everything is always wonderful? What I have learned through my journey is that in the greatest weakness, when I feel like my balloon/my body is going to burst, I choose to make decisions that are best for me and my family. It is in those moments when I have found my greatest strength and a confidence I never knew I had. Doing things you never have imagined doing, the difficult things, the hard choices, this is where my strength and confidence comes from and ultimately SUCCESS. In your darkest, weakest moments, when putting one foot in front of the other feels insurmountable, remember that on the other side of this pain is your power waiting for you to grab ahold of and fly to new heights of success, that you could never have imagined for yourself, your destiny. This is your time to SHINE!

About the Author, Alicia Hill-Marceau

Blog: http://peaches150.wordpress.com
Email: ahm2177@telus.net
Twitter: @ahm2177_alicia
Instagram: @peaches2177
http://www.facebook.com/alicia.hillmarceau

Alicia Hill-Marceau lives on Vancouver Island, BC with her two sons ages 12 years and 8 years old, and her husband of 17 years. Alicia has spent most of her life providing care for children starting as a babysitter and eventually turning her love of being with children into a career as a child care professional. Alicia ran her own Licensed Family Child Care for over 14 years until recently when she decided to retire to pursue her career further as a writer and author.

Alicia has already written one book entitled "Finally Me, Thanks to Vertical Sleeve Gastrectomy" and she has many more books to come. Alicia has always loved to write and it wasn't until she found her confidence that she decided that what she has was worthy enough to share with others. She knew that her struggle, being over 300 pounds, was one that many other people could relate to and she wanted to use her voice to let others know that they were not alone.

Alicia sees herself in the future sitting with Oprah under her Oak tree on Super Soul Sunday sharing more of her story and perhaps writing another book with people all around the world.

If you would like to contact Alicia for any reason please feel free to contact her at ahm2177@telus.net

If you have found this book to be helpful, I'd love to hear from you. Please take a moment to connect with me on Facebook here: http://www.facebook.com/alicia.hillmarceau

From Shock, Loss & Crushed Plans...How A New Path Developed Into A Successful Journey

By Holly Henbest

As a Realtor®, I partner with clients looking to buy or sell real estate in the greater Phoenix, Scottsdale and Paradise Valley communities. I partner with buyers to help them select and secure their dream home or investment property. When partnering with Sellers, our priority is to sell their home for the highest sale price possible, coupled with favorable terms and conditions, in the shortest amount of time possible.

For all of our clients, our goal is to ensure they have a professional, pleasant and fun experience, but most importantly we want them to feel informed and educated about the process and decisions that will be made along the way. We always tell our clients that they aren't just hiring us to do a job, but rather they are selecting us as their real estate partner.

We have been recognized for our success with awards and industry accolades, but the best reward is the expression of thanks we get from our clients. It is truly a thrill and an honor to help them achieve their real estate goals. Even better, we love it when a client comes back to work with us or when we receive a referral from a client. Not only is it meaningful to us personally, but it's the cornerstone of our business goals, and we are proud to say that over 90% of our business is repeat customers or referrals.

The Journey

So, how did I land in the world of real estate? When I was in college, I had my sights set on becoming a Realtor. It was my dream job! I loved homes and architecture and had once thought of becoming an architect. I also loved sales, marketing, negotiating, and working with people, and I pictured myself in a job that would allow me to be creative, would be challenging, would not tie me to a desk and would allow me to be out and about. Becoming a Realtor seemed like the perfect fit for all my personality, talents and goals.

Upon graduating from college, however, I quickly realized that I was not at a point in my life where I had the bankroll to start my own business. I had thought about the role but hadn't really considered the cost to start a small business. Additionally, I could not take on the risk of a career choice that offered no consistent paycheck or benefits. Therefore, I made the wiser decision to "learn the ropes" and start a career in a corporate environment.

I landed my first corporate position in the hotel industry, where I learned about sales, marketing, customer service and training. I learned from some very talented managers and ultimately managed my own departments and divisions. My last role in the hotel business was as the Executive Director of Sales and Marketing.

I then transitioned into the staffing industry and was soon relocated from San Diego to Arizona, where my goal was to increase sales and expand the operations in the greater Phoenix area. We were successful in our growth and along with that success came greater responsibilities. Some of those responsibilities included more frequent business travel. As business travel was increasing, I was juggling to balance my personal life as a single mom of a young son. Initially, I would take my son with me on business trips along with my mom who would accompany us, and she would be with him while I worked. When my son turned 3, the travel was increasingly becoming more difficult, and I realized that change would be necessary. I could also see that as my son grew older, I wouldn't be able to be the kind of mom I wanted to become if I stayed in this career path. I wanted to go to his school and sports events, drive carpool, and be a classroom mom. Between the travel and long hours, the corporate lifestyle was not conducive to my desired mom goals. I also knew that my job was no longer fueling me with the passion I had once. It was time for a new career. I wanted my career to fit my personal life goals and fuel me with a new passion.

On my 39th Birthday, I had lunch with a friend and was candid with her about my dwindling passion for my job and desire to change careers. As we chatted about what my next move would be – it hit me! I reflected back on my initial dream to be a Realtor. I was immediately fueled with that feeling of passion that I had been missing, and the timing seemed so perfect. At the time (2005), the real estate market was incredibly "hot." Residential real estate was booming with prices and volume of transactions escalating and new construction on what seemed like every corner.

The Birthday Present to Myself

After a year of planning, I made the transition into real estate the week of my 40th Birthday. It was the perfect birthday present! At last I was doing what I had always dreamed of doing! I had my sights set on building a successful business and experiencing motherhood the way I had always pictured. It was going to be perfect!

When I had first announced my intentions to change careers, the response from family and friends was overwhelmingly supportive, but there was a tinge of concern. I often heard – "Wow, you'll be great at that. We're so excited for you", often followed by "Do you really know what you're getting into? There's no paycheck, and there's no benefits, and you're a single mom, and that's a big risk."

During my year of preparing for the change I did a lot of homework and research to be sure I knew what I was getting into, but the reality was I didn't fully know.

My whole life I've been a risk taker. I'm a "go big or go home" mentality with a "go for it and make it happen" attitude. Even though I had done research, I mostly just knew that I would make it work. I had a history of creating sales and marketing departments and building businesses, and this would be no different...just a different industry. I was ready. I didn't want to let any more time slip away. It was time to seize the moment and follow my passion.

April Fool's Day was my official first day as a licensed Realtor. Who knew the joke would be on me. Hindsight today tells us that the climate of the real estate business then was beginning to change; in 2005 things had been in a frenzy, but in 2006 things were starting to take a turn. Unfortunately, no one had a crystal ball, and no one seemed to really know how significant the turn was going to be. I think that everyone initially thought that we were looking at a 'blip' in the economy. No one really seemed to fully see the writing on the wall of what was to come.

Shock and Loss

Just as I was getting my footing in the business and ready to forge ahead, my family was struck by a tragic loss. My mother passed away suddenly and extremely unexpectedly. To give you some idea of the circumstances, our family had just been on vacation, and my mom had literally been boogie-boarding the day before she collapsed. As I was driving home from the vacation, I received a call from my dad that my mother was being rushed to the hospital in Southern California. I immediately turned around to be at her side and learned that she had experienced a brain hemorrhage and would not survive. Obviously, there is never a good time to lose a loved one, but my mom was only 60 years old with all indications being that she was in perfect health. This was totally unexpected. My mother and father had their home in San Diego, and my sister, my son, and I spent a good amount of time there with my dad right after she passed. It took a long time just coping with the shock of our loss. There are no words that adequately describe it, but we were devastated.

The Financial Crisis

The several months after her passing are mostly a blur. I was so distracted by grief and emotionally supporting my family that I didn't have the focus needed to give my business the proper launch. By the time I started to really get it together and get going with business planning to a meaningful degree, it was mid-2007, which was when things overall in the economy and in real estate really started to take a turn for the worse. I felt sucker punched. First I lost my mom, and now the economy is crumbling.

Although the economy was downturning, we were still getting our business off the ground. We were so excited and proud every time we got a transaction into escrow, but then deals started falling apart in escrow. Appraisals started coming in low and in some cases loans were cancelled because the lending bank would go out of business right before closing. No loan meant no sale. It seemed like one thing after the next was going wrong. I was getting to the point where I thought, "Have I made a bad decision here? I am a single mom responsible for my son. I need to make a living." I had been so passionate and excited about this career, and it seemed like everything around me was falling apart.

Even when things seemed rough, I kept going. I remained focused to grow the business and be successful. I assumed the economy couldn't get any worse. Not only was my career on shaky ground, but my entire family was impacted. My dad joined me in the business in 2007 after relocating to Arizona. He had a rough time selling his home in San Diego. He and my mom had just remodeled and upgraded the house and then the prices took a sharp nose-dive. He also remained optimistic though and was excited to forge a path in a new career and a fresh start after losing my mom.

Then came 2008. Now we were at the real start of the crash. Not only was our real estate business on shaky ground, but my sister was also impacted, as she was working on Wall Street for Bear Stearns and it was the first bank to go down. So, we were all in what felt like a massive financial downward spiral.

As one bank after the next went down and the daily news was splashed with stories about government bailouts, I was reevaluating my career change. I felt fortunate to get calls from colleagues in my prior industry to see if I wanted to come back. I also considered new industries to transition into and part-time supplemental jobs. I thought about getting a job at Starbucks to get the benefits or my son's elementary school as an aide to just make a few bucks. I had many days where I thought I had made a huge mistake and really worried about what I would do. The worry was consuming and exhausting. At one point I was in serious talks with a company to return to a corporate position. I was about ready to negotiate my compensation package, and then my heart just sank. I realized that as hard as my situation was, this career in real estate was what I wanted, and I was going to do everything possible to make it work. I wasn't going to let my grief and the economy take me down. There were many sleepless nights and lots of worry.

Frankly, I was terrified, but I was a mom of a beautiful little boy, and I needed to take care of him. I would look into his eyes and know I had to make our lives better, and I was going to make everything okay for us.

The Plan

When I think about that time, I mostly reflect on my mental state and how I persevered. If it weren't for my mental fortitude, there is no way I could have continued. However, you can't "wish" yourself successful. You also have to have a plan. It's sort of a "what comes first" situation, "the chicken or the egg." For me, the attitude gave me the ability to create a plan.

Say It, Believe It

I adopted several mantras that I focused on daily, and I still do today.

"If you do the right things, the right things will happen." I remember thinking this mantra as I went to bed at night, woke up in the morning, and throughout the day. Thinking and saying it weren't enough though. I truly believed it…to my core. I believed that if I did the right things, then everything would be okay. Turns out I was right. Our clients' needs and goals were always the priority, and we always did the right things for them, and we turned out to be okay.

"Do what you love, and love what you do." This was, interestingly, my second most important mantra. Interesting because my primary mantra was about our clients and the second mantra was about me. Again, we always put our clients first. This mantra was also important because this is what I wanted to role model for my son. Although he was young, I felt it was important for him to have a mom who was following her passion. I wanted him to know it's important to listen to his heart and his head and do what he feels is right for him. Fingers crossed my role modeling works!

"You get what you give." For as long as I can remember, this is something I believed. Similar to "what goes around, comes around," but I took this to a different level. As we were facing difficult times, it was critical to come up with ways to feel better emotionally. Something that always makes me feel better is to give. People often feel that when you help someone or give a gift, the giver feels even better than the receiver, and I agree. When I was having a rough day or days and feeling more stressed than usual about cashflow, I would come up with a way to give something. I wasn't in the position to give financially, so I would give in other ways. I would go through my house and determine what I no longer needed that someone else might need. I would load up my car and deliver items to a charity. I would look for opportunities to donate my time to help charitable organizations and especially looked for opportunities to include my

son in our charitable efforts. Miraculously, each time we did this, it was like a boomerang effect of something good happening for us.

These mantras are all fairly common or cliché, but I believe there is a reason for that…they work. They worked for me! I was able to keep my head in the game and create a game plan to stay in business and potentially and hopefully grow the business.

Here to Help

That game plan required us to be nimble and flexible enough to see where change was needed in our business strategy. Sales were down. Prices were down. So many people were depressed and worried. We took a look at the situation and thought of where we might be able to help. That was really our goal - where can we still help? Where can we make a difference?

We then decided to transition our business to focus on short sales because so many people needed help with that. My dad was growing his role in the business; he was formerly an accountant with a significant background in financial accounting, taxation, and corporate treasury experience involving banking relationships, so it was smart to use his talents in managing our short sales. He could put together better than anyone else I know our clients' personal financial information and lay out the proper picture to present to the banks to ensure that a short sale would get approved. The industry needed quality solid Realtors to assist people at a time many were facing financial crisis and the most difficult time in their life.

We sat with people at kitchen tables and heard many tearful stories. No one goes into buying a home thinking someday I'm going to short sell it or face foreclosure, and in most cases, they were not only facing a real estate crisis, but they had additional issues – job loss, health issue, divorce or some sort of personal setback. The emotional pain was significant. Many felt their lives were falling apart around them and did not know what to do. We answered questions; we gave them information; we were there to help them.

There were many times when I was having a hard day and would meet with a client who would break down in tears and tell us their story. I had to realign my mindset and realize what my role was. My role was to help them, and I had to focus on them, not me. That experience, as difficult as it was, is a significant component to our continued success. I learned the importance and impact of home ownership. Not only is a home typically someone's biggest investment, but it's also a source of pride and reflection of their success.

In addition to our focus on short sales, we stayed disciplined. Having previously been in sales management, I know that activity breeds results, so we stayed active in connecting with potential clients. We also continually asked ourselves: *Who can I help today? Who can I talk to today? What can I do to grow myself, grow our business and help our clients?* We were consistently striving to be better and do more.

Lessons Learned, Goal Setting & Giving

Although we survived and did continue to grow our business, ultimately, it took the market recovering to enable us to truly flourish. During the period of the crash and recovery, we were building our reputation, such that when the market recovered we were respected, and people knew we were ethical, hard-working, problem solvers and results focused.

Many of our friends and clients often ask, "Don't you wish you had waited to become a Realtor after the crash?" While that may have been easier, I can say I have no regrets. The turmoil, stress and worry all contributed to my success and growth, not only in business but as a person.

That experience has made me a better Realtor, mom, daughter, sister, friend and neighbor. From a business perspective, I know that I can never get complacent. I am always researching and exploring ideas to ensure we are improving, learning and growing. It is critical to be nimble and flexible, in addition to pro-active, creative and thoughtful about directing your business planning and goals.

When it comes to goal setting, our business goals have never been about how many houses we sell or how much volume we produce. Our business goals have always been focused on how to improve our business and offer our clients the best experience and results. The goals are all about our clients and what they need. If you were to ask me today how many homes I've sold or how much volume we've sold…I don't know the answer. That doesn't really matter to me. Are we doing a good job, are we growing, are people referring people to us, are we creating record breaking results? That is what matters to us, and our goals are a reflection of that.

As I stay focused on those goals, I am extremely organized with to-do lists. Lists are like mini-business plans that are given constant attention. My lists include daily tasks in addition to short and long term projects. While I stay in the present with what needs to be accomplished today, this week and month, I am also always adjusting long-term goals. Some business owners make an annual plan, but I believe business moves too fast for an annual plan. Instead, I stay flexible and nimble by being open to constant re-evaluation.

While lists help me to stay organized and focused on priorities, they also give me an emotional boost. Having a list gives me a feeling of control and assurance that I'm not forgetting anything. They also keep me grounded to focus on priorities and prevent procrastination. Procrastination, I believe, is a business killer. I believe the faster and better I get something done, the faster and better our business will grow. Lists keep me motivated, and I absolutely love to cross items off the list. When I cross something off the list, I feel excited about the accomplishment. I have an internal joy meter that goes off with every item crossed off.

I also continue to be a risk taker. I like to experiment with new marketing opportunities and technology enhancements. Some work and some don't, but I'm willing to give things a try and then evaluate the success and learn from the failures.

Personally, the roller coaster economic ride made me very empathetic to others. Some have accused me of being "too giving" or "generous," and I know that is rooted in the experience of so many of us going through such a tough financial crisis. I just have an internal desire to help people and the mantras never stop – "Get What You Give" and "Do the Right Things" are on a constant loop running through my head.

The act of giving has also changed within our immediate family. We love to celebrate holidays and birthdays, and prior to 2008 our gift giving to one another was fairly lavish. After my mom passed away and then the market crashed, emotionally and financially the big gift giving just didn't make sense or feel good any more. Instead, we shifted our focus to giving experiences or spending time together. Today, we continue to spend money on doing something together such as a vacation or buying tickets to go to a sporting event, instead of buying a thing. This year for my son's birthday I'm giving him concert tickets, and we'll go to a concert together. When times were financially tough, we realized how much we didn't need, and we couldn't waste money on anything unnecessary. That turned out to be a blessing in disguise, because we are much more thankful to be creating memories, instead of buying things that we really don't need.

Bucket List

Something else we did to focus on creating memories was to create an activity bucket list. When money was tight, we couldn't afford a lot of extras, but we came up with a list of things we wanted to see and do that were budget friendly. We wrote these things down on slips of paper and put them in a jar. When we had a day available to do something fun, we pulled something out of the jar and off we went. Some of the items in the jar included going to see sights in Arizona (no expense involved besides gas), and this activity, in particular, was also beneficial to my job as it made me more

40

knowledgeable about my state. Other budget friendly activities that my son was particularly excited about included checking out unique donut, ice cream or candy shops. We even did a free tour of a candy factory. One summer we created separate jars: one for day trips, one for local sights and one for restaurants. Depending on our time availability, we would select from the appropriate jar. Knowing that we would be carving out time to do something fun helped to keep my mindsight more positive. We still continue to "bucket list" as often as we can. I've always believed that you should always have something to look forward to. Whether it be a vacation, night out with friends or a manicure…just knowing that you have something to look forward to helps to keep you in a more positive mindsight.

Thankful

Being thankful, I have also learned is important to focus on. During my many sleepless nights of worry and stress, I tried to remember I had a lot to be thankful for - our health, a roof over our heads, a new client. I was especially thankful for my family. My son kept me grounded and determined and also gave me reasons to smile, laugh and take breaks to enjoy and experience his childhood. Although times were tough, we had a lot of fun. We didn't take vacations for several years, but we created some great memories.

My dad and I were in it together and really relied on one another personally and professionally. We've continued to be a great balance of talents in the business. My sister provided emotional support and has been a great sounding board throughout the duration of our business. She also really understood the stress, since she also had to deal with her job loss from the Bear Stearns collapse and eventual relocation from New York to California.

In addition to my family, I've been lucky enough to have a great tribe of girlfriends who are supportive and fun. Being a single parent, it was especially important for me to have some adult time with friends and other moms.

Having family and girlfriends whom you know love you and are there to give you a hug or take you out for that glass of wine when you need it was incredibly important. As an independent, strong, and successful person, it has always been really hard for me to ask for support or help, but I needed them, and they were there for me. My advice to myself and others – ask for help when you need it. We're all in this together, and people love to help, so let them.

I'm also in this business together with professionals who are an extension of our business. Over the years I've been lucky to establish relationships with great people who also support us and our clients. There are several spokes in the wheel of real estate and to keep things rolling forward in the right direction, you need support from other talented individuals and organizations, including managing brokers and brokerages, mortgage lenders, title & escrow officers, inspectors, repair people, insurance providers and many more. I'm so thankful for the strong business relationships that we have developed.

All of these relationships, family, friends and colleagues, continue to inspire me and support our business and I'm so thankful for them and their contributions. They say "it takes a village" and we've created a wonderful village.

The Future

We look to the future with a great deal of excitement. Our business has flourished and we've added a third member to our team. As we grow, our goal is not to be the biggest but to be the Best. Luckily that goes along with our slogan – Partner with the Best! The Henbest Team!

Ultimately, no matter what life throws at you it's all about how you choose to react to it. As much as you can plan and make good decisions, it's always the unexpected events that shake up your life the most. Every person will have their own unique way to deal with adversity. When dealing with adversity, realizing you're not alone and knowing that others have also faced adversity and survived will hopefully help.

Find your passion.

Follow your dreams.

Be a role model.

If you do the right things, the right things will happen.

Do what you love and love what you do.

You get what you give.

Be nimble and flexible.

Stay disciplined.

Set goals.

Make lists.

Take risks.

Create a village.

Be generous.

Create a bucket list.

Be thankful.

About the Author, Holly Henbest

Realty ONE Group
Scottsdale, AZ
Mobile: 480-266-8785
Email: holly@henbest.com
Website: www.Henbest.com
Facebook: The Henbest Team
Instagram: Holly Henbest
Linked In: Holly Henbest
Twitter: @HollyHenbest
Snapchat: Holly Henbest

Holly Henbest is a Realtor with more than 25 years of sales, marketing, and client service experience. Holly's real estate accomplishments have been recognized with awards from the

Scottsdale Association of Realtors, Phoenix Business Journal, Top Agent Magazine and Arizona Woman Magazine.

Prior to her career in real estate, Holly graduated from San Diego State University and enjoyed a career in Sales & Marketing, working in the hotel and staffing industries. She relocated from San Diego to Arizona in 1996, after accepting a promotion to manage the Greater Phoenix market. Ultimately, she followed her passion for real estate, and dream of building her own business, and became a Realtor in 2006.

As a long-time resident of the Phoenix/Scottsdale area, she provides valuable insight on the community and its neighboring areas. She believes in building client relationships based on trust, integrity, and timely communication, and is honored to serve her clients and help them achieve their real estate goals.

Due to the depth of her experience and the breadth of her knowledge of the Phoenix real estate market, Holly appears regularly on a weekly television news segment for NBC 12News in Arizona, providing real estate information and insight.

Holly's real estate success has earned her numerous awards and accolades including:

Ranked #1 2016 - North Scottsdale Realty One Group
Top Agent - Top Agent Magazine - April 2016
Expert Network Distinguished Realtor Designation – 2016
100 Most Influential Real Estate Agents in Arizona – 2016
Top 100 Real Estate Agents in Scottsdale – 2016
Top 150 Real Estate Agents in Scottsdale - North Scottsdale
Magazine - 2017
Scottsdale Association of Realtors Top Producer - 2012, 2013, 2014,
2015, 2016
Co-author – How to Buy and Sell Real Estate in Today's Market –
2016
Co-author – Real Estate Game Changers – 201

The Wounded Healer

By Dr. Suzanne Sykurski

Dr. Suzanne is a gifted healer and licensed naturopathic physician. She is a very loving person who strives to be fully present for her patients and listens to them, as they tell their stories, from the depths of her soul. She relies on her medical training, experience, intuition, and her "God downloads" as she calls them, to truly understand the root cause of her patients' dis-ease. She inspires her patients to open up to her and reveal their true inner selves. She is non-judgmental and shares her own life, family, and health struggles to help her patients understand that they are not alone in their challenges. Her patients feel comfortable and safe with her. Many times, she has been told: "You're the first person I've ever told this to." Dr. Suzanne honors this trust and rapport between herself and her patients. She is gifted every day when a patient enters her clinic space, and together they explore life, health, motivations, fears, expectations, and challenges.

Dr. Suzanne laughs when she says that her style of practicing medicine is unique. She is cozy and warm and treats her patients like family when they become part of her practice and work with her over time.

She does not see any dis-ease as insurmountable. "You just need to figure out what it is, and what to do next (treatment)." Some of her patients have called her the "Dr. House" of naturopathic medicine. She has also been called the Sherlock Holmes of medical diagnostics. It is not uncommon for her to get a new patient who's seen to 5-15 doctors prior to her, trying to get answers and relief for their dis-ease or discomfort. "Look," she says, "all I really need to do is listen to the patient. The answer is in their story."

She has a high success rate in healing her patients…. but she warns that it will take very hard work, and a firm and unwavering commitment from the patient. There is no "one pill, one size fits all approach." The patient must do the hard work. She will hold their hands along the way, but she cannot "poof" a magic cure. She winks and says, "I wish I could, but what would be the purpose or the life lesson for that individual person? Going through our life challenges and achieving victory is how we grow and spiritually mature as individuals. It is part of our actualization process."

I took the forks in the road. The roads less travelled

I have had several different careers so far in my life's journey.

- I went to college and got a chemistry degree
- I did academic research and wrote an undergraduate research thesis
- I went into the Army after college as a Lieutenant and served overseas
- I worked in scientific research for the FDA as a toxicologist
- I went into the Army Reserves and served actively for 11 years
- I worked as a forensic chemist for a local police department in Maryland
- I went back to school and got a master's degree in chemistry and biochemistry
- I worked as a forensic chemist and toxicologist for the department of defense
- I went back to school again to pursue a doctorate in naturopathic medical education
- Today, I own a boutique naturopathic medical practice.

Early life: the wounded child

My early formative years shaped the adult I was to become. They were challenging. I was told that I was a very unhappy infant. I screamed and cried almost continuously for the first year of my life. They could find nothing to soothe me. I would lie awake at night refusing to close my eyes and go to sleep.

Very young, I had repeated bouts of illness. Every winter I was sick. I was always at the doctors for one thing or another. I was given antibiotics every time I went to the doctors.

My father was in the Navy and was gone for 6 years on an aircraft carrier. My mom was a basket case and could not handle raising us alone. She spent those years drinking Scotch every day with other Navy wives. We were left to fend for ourselves at the pool for most of the year. We lived in Southern California, so we had warm weather most of the year.

Every time I had to get vaccinations, I got very sick with fever, headaches, and severe fatigue. Moving overseas for 3 years in my childhood made my life interesting, but it came with lots of annual vaccinations. My poor little body did not do well with all these shots. Living overseas, I had to deal with a myriad of bacterial infections, viruses, and parasites.

Neither of my parents was emotionally demonstrative with love. Neither of them knew how to nurture. Many times, I felt like a little adult in a kid's body trying to figure out what to do.

I was very emotional and sensitive. My parents would not have any of that. If I was crying or upset, I was banished to my room to cry it out. I had to figure out how to calm down on my own. I was usually hoarse and exhausted by the time I calmed down; usually 1-2 hours later.

I was physically, mentally and emotionally abused by both of my parents. The abuse did not stop until I left for college. I was always reminded that I was a bad person.

My sisters constantly came on the attack against me. They were a unified force. They taunted me mercilessly until I broke down; they were evil to me and got very good, getting me into a complete rage. I would fly off and physically go after them. My punishment would be a severe beating from my mother. It consisted of face slapping, punching, pulling my hair, or fingernails dug deep into my arms that caused bleeding from the 4 puncture wounds. My dad's approach was punching me or kicking me in the back. He even used an electric cord from a blow dryer as a belt.

We moved 10 times during my father's 20-year Navy career. I lost friends almost every summer when I was in elementary school. The summer season is when we would move again. Every time, my parents would take our cat to the pound/SPCA. We had a different cat every year. My cats were the only living things that I loved and cherished. They were thrown away each year like cleaning out the garage.

I got Lyme disease. I was put on antibiotics for a short time. I could not walk down stairs for over a year and had to lift my body up using handrails for each step down. I had to stop running and could not do any exercise that involved using my knees.

Be careful what you say to a child

I was a deep thinker and tried to process things that didn't make sense to me. Many things about life and people confused me. Throughout my life, I was asked: "What is wrong with you?" Translation: There's something wrong with me. I'm defective. It's not OK to be sad. It's not OK to have strong feelings. It's not OK to be me.

I was a chunky kid. At a young age, my mother said to me "Oh, you'll never be tall and thin. You'll always be short and dumpy like your mother. You will always have a problem with your weight." Translation: I'm doomed to be fat! And there's nothing I can do about it.

I did not feel pretty around other girls. My mother told me: "You don't have the classic type of beauty that the boys your age are attracted to. You'll never be popular with the boys your age. Older men will appreciate you for the looks you have." Translation: I'm unattractive. I'll never be pretty and popular. I might as well give up on finding a boyfriend. My only chance is to get an older man one day who will love me.

I would process my ideas or questions at the dinner table. One family member or another would jump on me verbally at dinner. "What is wrong with you? Oh, Suzie.. (mocking, eyes rolling)." I was mocked in front of my family, by my family. I was mocked in public. I was the family scapegoat. It was so bad that a couple of boyfriends refused to come to my house for dinner because of the way I was mocked by them. The sad thing is, I never even noticed it. I really didn't. The mocking and verbal denigrations had become so common place that it was normal for me.

My mother told me: "I love you because I have to because you're my child. But I don't like you." Translation: I am not lovable. I am a bad person.

My grades were never good enough for my mother. She told me she "expected" me to get straight A's. She expected me to get a high grade on the college entrance exam. I did neither, and she was very disappointed in me. She criticized me and told me that I wasn't trying hard enough. Now I would never get into a good college.

Coping through perfectionism

I got through most of my childhood and young adult years by stuffing my emotions. I found out that mind-altering substances can help you forget about what you're sad about. Under their influence, I would laugh, be happy, feel connected to other people.

I became an overachiever to feel good about myself and to try and win my parents' approval. School and learning were my refuge. I LOVED to learn! I was a good student in school and got good grades. I worked very hard in school, always seeking perfect scores.

I lost myself in relationships. As long as I was with a boy, I felt loved and wanted. I never had many long-term relationships. My relationships were usually stormy and never lasted long. I was left devastated and despondent at the end of every relationship.

Music was very uplifting for me. Music could be ecstatic for me. I played it loud, and all the time. I went to concerts throughout my high school and college years. I danced my heart out to music. I would go to a night club and dance all night long.

I chose Chemistry, a very rigorous and demanding college education. I think I chose it because it was one of the hardest and I could prove my self-worth. I joined ROTC in school to push myself, again, looking for acceptance and validation from my parents. If I was to become an Army officer, I was sure they would approve and respect me.

I went to Army Airborne school. I completed my paratrooper training, though I was deathly afraid of heights and still am to this day. I wanted those airborne wings shining proudly on my uniform.

I went from not being able to run a city block to running 6 miles within a year. Running forced me to give up cigarette smoking. Trying to run and breathe was very painful for my lungs. From that year on, I made sure I excelled in Army standards of fitness. I got a perfect score in physical fitness tests for the next 16 years.

I went on Active duty after college and moved back overseas for 3 years. I was driven to perfection and excellence, so I was a good fit for the military. I took on some very challenging assignments and did my best to shine. As an officer, only perfection is acceptable.

Finding My Way to Wholeness

I worked very hard to get my health and my life in order over the years. I went through years of psychotherapy, sorting out my depression, anxiety, and low self-esteem. I had to face my issues of childhood abuse. I conquered alcohol addiction and held on to my accountability buddies in AA for dear life.

I went to every alternative healer I could find within a 50-mile radius.

I was introduced to the mysterious shadow world of alternative medicine. I did energy healing, bodywork, herbal therapies, homeopathic therapies, went to seminars and read over a hundred books on natural healing. I meditated, sometimes over an entire weekend. I trained and became a Usui Reiki Master myself, so I could work on my self-healing at home.

I worked on my physical body by joining a gym, losing 30 pounds and 25% body fat. I became an amateur bodybuilder and a gym rat. I radically cleaned up my diet. I became a self-taught expert in nutrition and vitamin therapies.

I went back into the Army as a reservist. I wanted to make my amends and do a better job this time. I succeeded and got promoted twice over the next 11 years. I held a company command position and did the job to the best of my ability, with pride and purpose.

Then, it all hit the fan.

I Had to Crawl My Way Back

Nine years into my healing journey, I had a major setback involving alcohol, a car accident, and a co- dependent, unhealthy relationship I was in. I was so broken, and I couldn't face the mess I found myself in. The following night, instead of turning to my new-found resources of love and healing, I wanted to leave. Go Home. I cried all night for God to bring me home. I swallowed some pills, wanted to go to sleep, and wake up in heaven. I was so tired. I did not think I had the strength to continue to fight anymore. At 34 years old, I just could not do it anymore. Life was too damn hard.

Within 2 years, my life was back on track, with more levels and layers of healing. I was sober again, and have been for 22 years now. I was healing my emotional issues and could get off medication for depression and anxiety. My self-esteem was growing. I was happy, probably for the first time in my life. I had my friends, my support network, and my web of healers.

By this time, I was healing others with hands-on energy. I was blessed with the ability to heal with my hands. I helped women through PMS, migraines, and even PTSD from sexual abuse. I received the gift of medical intuition. I knew where people were hurting because I could feel it in the exact same place in my body. I had a powerful and profound connection with the animal kingdom. These were things that I could not explain with my analytical scientific mind. I surrendered. I accepted this as my new normal. I didn't make sense to me.

Little did I know that God had other plans for me

In 1997, I was offered a fully funded opportunity through my job to go back to school and get my doctorate in forensic toxicology.

At the same time, I received a strange little flyer in the mail about Bastyr University out in Seattle, WA. Two of their department deans were coming out to NIH in Bethesda, MD to do a recruiting gig. What the heck, why not go out there and see what they have to say?! I took the thunder out of their presentation because I was asking the very direct and serious questions. I needed to know that this was "legit." I lived around the military industrial complex of the D.C. area and naturopathic medicine as a licensable recognized field was not in the consciousness where I lived at the time.

I honestly had no idea what to do. I was being offered my "dream" career opportunity. My life was back on track, and I was happy. I did the healing I needed to do for now, and it was time to live my life. I was long overdue for this. I worked hard for this over the past 11 years. Couldn't I just go to festivals and health fairs and volunteer on the weekends? I was willing to do that.

I mentally tabled it for the time being. My plan was to become observant of the world and situations around me. I had odd, strange encounters with the animal kingdom, mainly black crows! Hundred at a time and they didn't come around just once. It happened frequently over a 12-month period. Strange, beautiful things were happening around me. I would have a surreal, unique experience, and then a sign, billboard, or conversation would take place about a topic related to natural healing. These "coincidences" did not seem like mere random coincidences anymore. I was excited and scared when I realized what I had to do next.

By the end of 1997, I applied to Bastyr for the Fall 1998 incoming class. Late spring, after I was accepted, I resigned at my DoD job for August. I tried to sell my cute little duplex starter home but was unsuccessful. I ended up renting it out. I flew out to Seattle to look for an apartment to rent share. I donated or gave away half of my belongings. I knew that my 2 kitties were DEFINITELY coming out to Seattle with me. It was an exciting time. A lot of my fears dissipated once the preparations and activities got rolling.

You're going to do WHAT?!

Very few people in my life supported my decision to quit my job and go back to school to study naturopathic medicine. My family, friends, professional colleagues, and co-workers were completely baffled by my decision. Everyone thought it was crazy and irresponsible to sacrifice a wonderfully successful career. And what was "naturopathic what?" Several of my co-workers were mumbling to others that I was "off my rocker," "going mental", or having a "midlife crisis."

My parents were very antagonist towards me for this decision. We went through periods of arguing and disagreements. My father's very first response was: "And how do you think you're going to pay for THIS? I'M not paying for this." I told him I was going to pay for this and that I had found a way to apply for student loans. I distanced myself from them during this time and kept a safe distance. Contact and communication was limited.

Sometime late that summer I was at a family member's party. I was talking to a woman, one of her neighborhood friends. Her reaction was, "Oh my gosh! I'm so jealous. You can just take off and start all over. You can go back to school and start a whole new life. You're free to do whatever you want. You aren't married, you have no children, nothing to hold you back. I'm stuck here. There's no way I can do anything like this." She was the first person to acknowledge what I was doing was positive. This positive affirmation came from a total stranger, and I was grateful that I met her that day.

A week before I was to leave, there was a knock at my door. It was my father.

Me: Who's there? (I could see him through the peep hole) Dad: It's me, can I come in?"

Me: What for?

Dad: I want to help you.

Me: Why do you want to help me?

*Dad: Can you please open the door and let me in? It's hot as **** out here.*

I opened the door and let him in. My father stood across from me, but could barely look me in the eye. I railed into him for how he was acting towards me. His answer, sheepishly looking down: "Because I'm jealous. I'm jealous that you have the courage to leave your job and follow your dream. I've never had the courage to do anything like that. You have the courage to stand up for what you believe in. My generation stayed in the same job for 30 years to get a retirement pension. You didn't dare leave your job. Once you had a job, you stayed in it no matter what."

The emotions settled down. For 4 days, we packed up boxes. My goal was to leave on Monday, Labor Day. We finished up by Saturday. We didn't say much to each other during the time. My father never said very much to me anyways. It was nice to have him there. It was a silent bonding for us.

On a Monday, I pulled out of my driveway with my packed up 16-foot truck, my 16-foot flatbed car trailer with my car on top, my two sedated cats in their carriers next to me, a cooler full of drinks and food, and self-help cassette tapes to listen to along the way. My journey out to Seattle was 3000 miles, 5 days of driving at 14 hours per day.

I had 2 weeks to settle in after I arrived. September 28, 1998, was the first day of the beginning of my new life. Six beautiful, grueling years of medical education, a marriage, and a baby. I graduated in 2004 with a husband, a beautiful 2-year-old boy, and a degree as a naturopathic medical doctor.

The path to healing is a lifelong commitment

The journey to get where I am today took my whole life. I have been working on my physical, mental, and emotional health for 31 years. Healing from childhood trauma never stops. I believe it is a lifelong process. If we stick to a healing path, we reach deeper levels and layers of healing. I would say that the first eleven years of healing and change were my most difficult.

I think it's important to find the right health providers. It's important to stick it out with someone for a year or two. If you think that someone is not right for you, it's very important to make sure that it's not just your reluctance to do what they are asking of you. Change is very difficult. Many times, we have to do things we don't want to do. Many times, change can be painful. I can get put off by an aggressive, in-your-face, provider. Most of the time, it's what I need. I need someone with strong boundaries.

My internal resources

Discipline, dogged determination, stubbornness, perseverance, and faith. I have a lot of courage and hope, though people usually saw these qualities in me long before I did. Early on, people who heard my story always told me that I was going to make it. They saw something in me I didn't see at the time. They gave me hope because I had little of it to give myself. Inside I was terrified and felt defeated.

Outside I showed strength and bravado. I don't think it was an act to put on the brave face. When I was in groups like AA meetings, I was brutally honest about how I was feeling.

I have always had a very strong connection to Spirit and to God. It was very powerful when I was a young Catholic. I fell in and out of my relationship with God over the years. Though I felt like I left Him, He never left me. I do believe now that He was been there all along pushing me in the right direction. He worked so hard on me, to get through my own stubbornness. God wants me to have victory. I became a baptized Christian in 2005.

My external resources

Psychotherapists, holistic health providers, group support meetings and relationships, exercise, meditation, and books on health and healing. I found friends who cared about me and were there for me. The healing gurus I sought help from were very instrumental in my healing. They gave me hope and a different paradigm from which to view my challenges. These women, and some men, were happy, calm, supportive, centered, at peace, nurturing and kind. They filled a role to parent me since I was not parented in love during my upbringing. They were my rock. If it wasn't for these wonderful healers, I probably would have never taken that final fork in the road to change careers.

I have a husband who rarely questions my next protocol. I have done so many healing protocols in the 17 years we've been together. Our kitchen counter is lined with 20-30 supplements at any one time. I am a master at creating protocols, many of them I create for myself. I have spent tens of thousands of dollars on my healing over the years.

My most powerful external resource is my son. Having my son and nurturing him the way I never was has been the most healing experience in my life. I found and experience unconditional love every day. He has been challenging over the years, but I never withdraw love from him. We are so much alike and think the same way. I am excited to see how his life will unfold and grow, as he has strong love and support from both of his parents, an amazing sense of self and very powerful self-esteem.

Mindset is very important to overcoming adversity

Mindset is CRUCIAL. I have discovered in myself over the years that when I make up my mind to do something, I will accomplish it. When I set defined goals, I meet them. Learning to deal with and overcoming adversity is what builds character and resilience. Having a growth mindset is the key to success. A growth mindset, as opposed to a fixed mindset, is the belief that you are in control of your own ability, and can learn and improve. Having that underlying belief that you are in control of your own destiny is more important than hard work, effort, and persistence.

With a growth mindset, we can view a setback as an opportunity to learn. We will try harder and do whatever it takes to overcome the problem. It is not just important for learning new skills. It can affect the way that we think about everything. With a growth mindset, we know we will recover from an illness because we believe that we can do something about the illness. We are no longer a victim, and we know we have control over our lives.

18 years ago, in 1999, I met a neuroscientist on a catamaran cruise in Mexico. It was during my first year at Bastyr. He was excited about the work I was doing, and that that I was a research scientist for many years. Even more excitedly, he told me about the work he was doing: he was studying neuroplasticity in a laboratory setting. They proved scientifically that brain cells (neurons) can re-grow and renew themselves. This was exciting news for the whole scientific and medical community. We thought up until this research that brain cells and brain cell function was fixed. We believed that brain cells could not regenerate once damaged. The rest of the body does every day, but we thought it was impossible for brain cells.

Tips for choosing success over adversity

Accept that adversity is inevitable in life

Adversity is part of life. To avoid or resist it will only make it persist. If we accept this, we can use adversity to challenge ourselves and use it as an opportunity to grow from. Our bodies are sustained from stresses continually, over our lifetime. Without stress, we would die. We need it for our neuro and intellectual development and growth. Plants will thrive and flower when under intermittent stress.

Get help from outside sources

You cannot do it alone. Human beings were not created to do life alone. We were created to help one another. Until you get the tools you need and the right mindset in place, your situation will keep perpetuating itself. Find a counselor who specializes in dealing with your current challenge. Find a health provider who specializes in the area of your health concern. Hire a life coach. Life coaches are very popular now. They can help with just about any challenge you are going through. They can help you set goals and keep you accountable.

Accept that you have the power to do something about it

Human beings are very powerful creators. Our thoughts are our most powerful tool. If we have a strong conviction that we can't do anything about a situation in our life, that we are a victim of circumstance, then we will stay in that situation. We will continue to draw to ourselves those things that will continually reinforce this mindset. The opposite is true. When we know we are in control of our situation, and that we can do something about it, then we will seek out those things that we need in order to change our circumstance in a positive way. We will draw to ourselves those people and situations that will help us turn things around in a positive way.

Look outside of yourself when your life situation is difficult

Volunteer. Reach out to another person. Lend an ear to someone who is struggling. We may think that we have so many problems that there is no way we can help another person. Not true! AA and other recovery groups work so well because these people hold each other up in their worst times and commend each other on their little successes. If you have a physical limitation and can use a phone, reach out that way.

Build your internal resources

Cultivate emotional strength, faith, courage and discipline. You can prepare yourself mentally for confronting adversity head-on. Often, when you're prepared for the worst, the worst never happens. Have faith that everything will work out. Pray. Find a power greater than yourself. Have faith that there is always light at the end of the tunnel, and faith that "this too shall pass." If your life has been destroyed by adversity and you don't have the ability to build your internal resources, reach out to someone who can help you.

Build your external resources

Surround yourself with a support system of family, friends, and allied professionals. We all need encouragement and support. We need each other. We need someone to talk to, someone to help ease the burden. Even just knowing a friend is there when you need them can be most comforting. Find a support group of people going through the same situation you are, whether it is emotional, an illness, or a financial situation.

Use positive affirmations

The power of repeated thoughts and words can be harnessed for creating positive change in our lives. Write down your affirmations. Write affirmations that are goal-oriented, in present tense and as though they have already been achieved. Don't just tell yourself what you want; act as though you already have it. Repeat your affirmations as often as possible. The more you repeat your affirmations and surround yourself with them, the deeper the message will be ingrained in your mind and absorbed into your subconscious. Tape your list of affirmations on your bathroom mirror. Read these every morning when you wake up and before going to bed.

Create a gratitude list
A gratitude list is used as an exercise to shift your mood and attitude. Making a gratitude list helps us to recognize these blessings and keep our focus on the good things in our lives. Creating and reading gratitude lists will help promote a positive attitude every day. It is a good tool to have to lift your spirits when you need a little lifting. It is a great way to start the day off on the right foot. Start out small. Think of 5 things that you are grateful for. You can add to this list over time.

I am woman, I am strong, hear me roar!

Using these various tools over the years have made me stronger. I did not have any hope that circumstances and situations in my life would ever change. It was most likely ingrained into my fixed mindset from a very young age. My parents told me so all the time. I believe that the most powerful message and hope that I got was from my conversation with my catamaran buddy back in Mexico. Neuroplasticity! Science proved that we change our brain, mentally, emotionally, and physically. Each little thing I did, each little victory that I had, helped me grow and heal in a positive direction. Even when I backslid, relapsed, and made my life a chaotic mess again, somewhere deep in my mind I knew I would overcome it. I did it before, and I can do it again.

Changes in how I approach life

My life, my circumstances, my victories, and my experiences have changed me. "I wish I knew then what I know today." Maybe. Sometimes I kick myself for not being where I think I should be. I get frustrated that I am not further along in certain areas of my life. The difference now is that I am learning to see that each new challenge, each new set back, is a new opportunity for growth. I am currently dealing with issues of chronic Lyme disease that resurfaced 2 years ago after being in remission for 2 decades. I was physically mentally and emotionally beat down during the first year. The second year, I turned this time into an opportunity to figure out how to heal myself. I spent the past year working on a comprehensive protocol for chronic illness. The "gift" of my Lyme disease created an opportunity to create the next phase in my medical practice. I turned a negative situation and life event into an opportunity for growth.

An important lesson I learned that still impacts my decisions today

I have a powerful force of intuition that lives inside of me. Throughout most of my life, I ignored what I was feeling as my "gut instinct." Repeatedly this strong intuition presents itself when situations arise that need to be carefully managed. I have learned to trust this intuition. When things are not congruent, and it involves another person, I have learned to speak my truth. It can be challenging and scary and has caused rifts in relationships. I have tried to avoid any form of conflict in my life for too many years. Using my intuition and speaking my truth has been liberating and is helping me to continue to grow as a person and as a professional.

Advice I would give to others going through a challenging time

Get out a writing pad. Write down what you are going through. Write it all out. Write about how it is affecting your life. Write out how bad it is. What parts of your life it has ruined. Spend as long as you need to finish this, but I would not take more than a week. Take what you wrote and bury or burn it in a fireproof bowl, a fireplace, or an outdoor grill. Let it go up in flames. Observe the horrible things in your life burning up and going up in smoke.

In a week, sit down and write out what you are grateful for in your life. You may even find yourself writing about aspects of your situation that you suddenly feel grateful for. Hold onto this. Read it every day for 7 days.

Visualize exactly how you want your life to be. Create a vision board with photos that illustrate these things you want in your life. Sit quietly. Calm your breathing. Relax. Think of all the ways your current situation could possibly be used as a catalyst for future growth.

About the Author, Dr. Suzanne Sykurski

www.alpinenaturopathic.com
alpinenaturopathic@yahoo.com
dr.s@alpinenaturopathic.onmicrosoft.com

Dr. Suzanne is a WA state licensed, board-certified Doctor of Naturopathic Medicine, scientist and researcher. She received her medical education from the world renowned Bastyr University in Seattle, WA. She has degrees in Chemistry (BS) and Biochemistry (MS) and worked professionally as a research and a forensic toxicologist. She served as a forensics expert witness for 11 years.

Dr. Suzanne has a deep empathy for the aches, pains and ailments of her patients. She herself has suffered many of the same afflictions as the patients who come to her today. She set about to study and learn how to heal herself of these conditions, first during her 15-year career as a research scientist and forensic toxicologist, then 13 years as a practicing physician.

Over the years, Dr. Suzanne has developed highly effective proprietary and copyrighted programs designed to help patients recover from many of the nagging conditions that baffle other doctors. Her unique, in depth scientific approach comes from her dedication to innovation and integrity. She takes the time to listen to her patients with compassion and care.

Dr. Suzanne's mission is to support and empower individuals to find answers to restore their health, increase vitality, and improve self-esteem.

Dr. Suzanne expanded her medical practice to work with patients out of state: via Skype, FaceTime, or phone (telemedicine). This has allowed her to reach out more globally to help people who are specifically seeking the expertise that she has.

Dr. Suzanne is married and has an awesome socially conscientious teenage son. Together they care for their small home zoo: 2 dogs, 2 cats, and 2 sugar gliders. They said goodbye last year to their patriarch cat and their ferret.
In her free time, she researches peer-reviewed medical journals, reads books on health-related topics, writes, brews kombucha, and practices amateur landscaping on their property.

Finding Happiness

By Alexandra Romann

As I sit here in my dining room, I look out into my sun-filled yard with the Pacific ocean and mountains in the distance, I feel happy, a feeling that still overwhelms me with a sense of disbelief. I glance over to the couch, where my husband Neal is sitting typing on his laptop. He looks good and healthy, focused on his work. My heart closes briefly as a memory of his pale face, empty eyes, and twitching body intrudes my thoughts. I take a breath and try not to engage with the recollection. Summer air fills the room, and in about an hour, the sound of little feet and laughter (or fighting) will surround me when our children return from a morning with their grandma. My heart opens again, and I feel a deep sense of gratitude for my life with my amazing family, having the means to afford travel and such a beautiful home, and getting to work from home on my own business. I truly love my business and the amazing people I get to help create more time, financial freedom, and happiness in their lives. It's a far cry from the corporate world I used to so desperately want to be a part of, a path through many years of post-graduate school that ended in a cubicle. Some days I can't believe that I'm in this place where I wake up excited for life.

The floor is littered with toys and stickers that were put there when I decided that it was not a battle I wanted to pick. I try to embrace most wonderful, exhausting, annoying, hopeful, loving, and funny parts of what my life has become because it's the perfect imperfect life I never knew would become a reality for someone like me. I say "most" because I also have those days, the ones where things just don't seem to flow. It's part of being human. I used to think that a life of happiness was reserved for a handful of lucky people who surely had no struggles, perfect health, and who probably owned a private island and diamond collection that they inherited from their parents. Except none of those things are a precursor to happiness. Everyone, every single person has struggles and the sooner we stop comparing, the better off we are. I believe the first step towards happiness is accountability. Once I started holding myself fully accountable for not only everything that I did, but also all the adversities that happened "to" me, my life slowly but consistently started to improve. I'll start at the beginning.

The beginning

I was born in Zurich, Switzerland, in the early 80s, in that gap right after the GenX and before the Millennial generations. Even though I was an only child, I never felt alone because all my friends lived within walking or biking distance and my parents were always available, with my mother being a stay-at-home mom. I had a great childhood and grand plans for the future, like owning my own hotel and most definitely getting a perm the minute my mom would allow it. Thankfully, by the time this became an option, perms were long a fad of the past. As I entered my teens, I was very independent thanks to a very well-established public transit system, our central location, and my amazing circle of friends. I was a good student and spent almost every day after school in some extracurricular activity. I leaned towards the arts and languages but didn't have a specific goal for what I wanted to do when I grew up.

It had been my parents' dream for a long time to move to Canada to open a pastry shop where my dad could pursue his initial expertise of being a pastry chef and chocolatier. After years of going through the application process, it was finally approved when I was 15. Was it a reality check? No. I was too young to understand this was more than just a fun adventure. So we left the only home I'd ever known.

It was hot and humid in Vancouver. We settled 5 hours towards the interior of the province, in a lovely house on a small lake surrounded by trees. It was 13 kilometres to the nearest bus stop, and I realized that my days of freedom were over. My parents worked long days in their business and had long gone to work by the time I got up to catch the school bus. I'd had one year of an English elective in school before our move. The fact that I could introduce myself and knew words like waste paper basket, chair, and table did not prepare me well for the high school I got placed in. It was the most lonely period of my life. I cried every single morning before school, put on my best face desperately trying to make some friends, and took breaks of silently crying in the school restrooms when the actions of those having fun at my expense got to me. I was painfully homesick and disliked everything about my new home. I missed my friends, my hobbies, my identity. I was drowning in my victim mentality and reinforced all the things that were happening "to" me by deeming myself helpless. By the time I reached university, I'd made a few close friends and was generally not unhappy; I wasn't particularly happy either. I loved the independence of owning my own car and the freedom of university courses. Despite speaking English fluently, I focused on the sciences and mathematics partially because I was searching for answers about anything and everything in nature and the universe. However, I had let the harshness of my high school experiences burn into my heart, and I found trusting people very difficult. It would take years for me to stop pushing people away out of fear of getting hurt.

Coasting through life

Most of my decisions in my early 20s were fear-based. I'd probably be sitting in a pant suit in some meeting somewhere in Toronto had I not met a handsome man one fateful afternoon while I was serving at a restaurant during a gap year between my bachelor and masters degrees. His free spirited attitude and sharp mind intrigued me, and his work ethic made the fact that he was a struggling entrepreneur somewhat acceptable to me. And by struggling I mean the no money, living in his parents' basement suite kind. He'd just lost all his savings in a business that he started and failed at. Yet he got up and tried again, with a determination I'd never seen in anyone before. Despite what my brain was telling me, my heart was hooked. He taught me more about consistency over the coming years than anyone: Consistency in his work, trying again after each failure, and consistency in how much he cared for me, loving me more each time I got scared. I finished my masters degree and got a job as a statistician analyzing health data. It was interesting and dynamic; I loved it but soon became restless as I wanted more. More leadership, more financial freedom. I figured that if I'd ever have kids, ideally I'd get to work while my future husband would stay home with them. I was determined to reach career success. Neal and I got engaged while on vacation and were coasting through life for a bit. Coasting is sneaky, in that it's not so bad that you have the desire to get out, but it's also not the key to happiness. Everything was fine, and we settled for that, not knowing that greatness was just out of our comfort zone.

The Adversity

In those early years, Neal and I always had to watch our money, and we'd often say, some day we'll experience this or get that. "Some day" was this magical time in the future where everything we'd ever dreamed of would have become a reality. We often talked about some day, until life gave us the biggest lesson and threatened to end life as we knew it.

Neal's disease started slowly and progressed quickly. It began with small cognitive problems and twitches in his limbs, and moved to him barely remembering any conversations or events; he was also having full-body tremors day in and out. Somewhere in the earlier stages, we had our beautiful wedding. It was a beautiful day filled with love and our friends and family. What they didn't know was that two weeks before we had gotten a diagnosis from Neal's neurologist. Well, it wasn't really a diagnosis, they just confirmed that the lesions in his brain were increasing rather quickly and that nobody knows the brain enough to conclude whether this would evolve into Multiple Sclerosis.

Neal's character started changing and I rarely heard him laugh anymore. He wasn't the same person I fell in love with and thinking about the future sent my anxiety through the roof. I often wanted to scream. I wanted children and a real marriage with this man. My career goals suddenly looked boring and a life in front of a screen seemed bleak. I wanted our life back and was filled with guilt and regret for not enjoying it to the fullest before. The fact that our future was no longer certain – not that it ever was – forced me to really think long and hard about what I wanted out of life. Neal's cognitive and nervous function declined so rapidly that he couldn't have a conversation without stuttering, he'd put the cheese in the freezer instead of the fridge, and his whole body would twitch. It all seemed so unfair, and all the things I wanted to experience with him, and maybe deep down thought I would one day, became very clear. My long hours at my job that I thought would get me ahead in my career no longer seemed like an honourable sacrifice. I suddenly saw the flaws in the way I was living my life, the lack of accountability and blaming of external sources that I would turn to whenever things did not go my way. But I didn't notice my biggest flaw. I isolated myself completely. I dropped many friends because I couldn't even bear being asked the innocent question of how I was doing. I shared the bare minimum about Neal's condition and completely separated myself, especially from those closest to me. Thankfully, many of our amazing friends stuck around and sadly, some didn't. I felt incredibly lonely and was sleeping just four hours a night in my worried state. Our finances suffered as Neal struggled to focus enough to get clients and my salary, while decent, didn't last very far in Vancouver. Meanwhile, the medical professionals were doing the best they could but didn't know the cause of the consistently increasing brain lesions. It was a dark time in both our lives.

The Turn-Around

Winter passed, and so did the one-year mark of the onset of Neal's symptoms. I went for coffee with an old school friend who was visiting from out of town. She was the first person to verbalize what many people surely were thinking: You don't look good at all! And just like that, although we weren't particularly close, it all spilled out of me. She recommended we go see a blood analyst who had helped her sister who had been very ill. I put Neal on the waiting list and in June we got a call that there had been a cancellation, so off we went on the 5-hour trip. It was a silent drive and fear of what the day would hold in store for us gripped our hearts with a chilling possibility. I won't go into the details of the appointment because of my lack of knowledge about the biology of it all. But the bottom line was that the cause of all of his symptoms including the lack of energy was caused by the inability of his red blood cells to do their job properly. Because of how quickly this was progressing, Neal's condition would only worsen unless he would follow the prescribed treatment exactly. Within about six weeks, he had a lot more energy, and the constant twitches of his body and head slowed down, and within about two months, his stuttering slowed down. By six months, many of his symptoms had been reversed, and within a year, almost all of his symptoms were gone. This was all accomplished with a very specialized regimen of different supplements, a few dietary changes of what not to eat, and avoiding stress. There is no doubt in my mind that the blood analyst saved Neal's life. He was still seeing his neurologist, and after following the blood analyst's protocol, another MRI showed that he wasn't getting any more lesions in his brain. His symptoms never returned.

The Rollercoaster

I'd love to tell about how our life has been absolutely perfect since then. In many ways it has, and in some ways it's been difficult. Many of the things we set out to achieve when Neal was so ill did become our reality. With our new lease on creating a life together, we were determined to not stress the small stuff and follow our hearts. Neal got his business up and running again, and we moved to a small seaside town just outside Vancouver. I was soul-searching, trying to find what I wanted to do with my life. I hadn't found it yet, but what I did find was unconditional love as we were blessed with our beautiful daughter.

When she was just a baby, Neal was diagnosed with an autoimmune arthritis. His knees get very inflamed and many everyday tasks are painful. There were times when he couldn't walk. A sobering condition for someone whose number two love in life is snowboarding (I presume that the kids and I take the number one spot). No matter how tough things got with his pain, he never ever gave up. His resilience is admirable, as he followed diet after diet with astounding discipline in search of finding healing. Most of the pain and inflammation relief was achieved by avoiding sugar, dairy, grains and starches. He currently follows this diet in addition to light stretching and exercise, chelation therapy, avoiding stress, and the removal of his amalgam fillings. It has not been easy all the time, but our love for each other and our family, what we've overcome, Neal's dedication to his health and business, and our joint path of personal development has made us happier, more fulfilled, and excited for the future than we've ever been. I truly love my life, my family, and my friends. I'm still on the rollercoaster but have found a passion for life that has displaced the fear. And with fear being mostly out of the picture, its other expressions such as guilt, blame, and envy also packed their bags.

How we make it through adversity

We made a decision a long time ago, when Neal was really ill, to bring positivity into our lives and minimize any negative impact. For us, this meant not watching the news (thank you, internet!), spending less time with the complainers and blamers, and starting our day with something positive. This has evolved over time. We had started with some exercise and now do our best to roughly follow the Miracle

Morning. We have two young children and sometimes our miracle morning is actually snuggles with our babies or a mad rush getting out the door after accidentally turning off the alarm in a sleep-deprived state.

The perfectionist in me could never be happy; I've had to reprogram my thinking to find happiness in progress. It's a journey, and if we learn to look at adversity as a teacher, I truly believe we can overcome it. The problem is that it's easy to believe that when things are going well, it's when things get tough that we often feel like giving up on the person, situation, business. Consistent daily personal development, especially in the form of books and audiobooks, changes the mindset, and I believe this is the single most important piece of advice I've ever gotten in my personal development journey, because when you better yourself you automatically better your circumstances. I'm a better wife, a better mom, a better friend, a better daughter, a better entrepreneur, a better human being because of everything I've gone through and learned. Adversity accelerates growth, that's why it's so painful sometimes. Without it, I'd probably still be stuck in my tiny box, worrying about all these little things that don't matter.

The second most important factor that helps us through adversity is exercise. Doing the personal development should automatically result in a desire to keep the body healthy. I'm the first to admit I don't get the cardio I should. Progress.

Another outcome from personal development is being aware of the feeling of gratitude. Happiness precedes success and gratitude precedes happiness. In other words, it all starts with being thankful. The more I focus on what I'm grateful for, the happier I become, which results in better friendships, better family dynamics, increased opportunity, and more business. Initially, I didn't really believe this, but I gave it a shot.

I've realized that it really takes a village. My biggest mistake was my pulling back from people and not sharing or nurturing friendships because I was so wrapped up in our own grief. And yes, it was horrible, but at the same time, I became a horrible friend. Maybe they were going through something too and they needed me, but I just wasn't there for them because I was so wrapped up in my own life and constantly feeding that negative loop of fear, worry and anxiety. Lesson learned.

Choosing Success

Success, to me, is happiness in all areas of life. Going through adversity has not only made me stronger, but it has also made me a happier person because I'm so grateful that I get to be with this incredible man and for the life we've created. Choosing happiness has allowed us to become healthier, energized, and more successful.

I guess my biggest advice is to not wait for things to "fall into place" to live life. For too long I thought that something in the future, better job, better finances, better relationships, success, would allow me to be truly happy and to live a life of fearlessness. Nobody needs to wait for a wakeup call to step out of their comfort zone. Regardless of spiritual views, I think we all hope to live the happiest and best life possible. Life is happening right now, with all its imperfections and fragility.

About the Author, Alexandra Romann

Website: www.alexandraromann.com
Email: alexandraromann@yahoo.ca
Facebook: https://www.facebook.com/alexandra.romann
Instagram: https://www.instagram.com/alexandraromann

Alexandra Romann is a dedicated wife and mother who has created more time freedom and happiness by following her heart and never giving up. She lives with her husband and two young children in a small seaside town on the west coast of British Columbia, Canada. As a statistician in the health sector, she always enjoyed being able to make a difference in people's lives. After finding her passion that allows her more time with her children, she now strives to empower others to gain more time freedom and becoming a more fulfilled, happier, and better version of themselves. To get to know her better, see a list of her recommended books, or work with her, visit her website, one of her social media channels, or get in touch with her directly. She loves meeting new people and helping others create more freedom to choose the life they want to live.

Rural Upbringing

By Carrie Ware, CPA, CA.

I originally became an accountant because I wanted a career that would be relatively free from economic downturns, as people and businesses would always need tax advice, bookkeeping, accounting and tax filing. Once I started working with clients, I realized that I had the ability to help them find solutions by breaking their problems into smaller issues that were then easier to solve. Early on in my career as a junior accounting student, I enjoyed being able to help clients. Then as a junior CA at the Merritt firm, I found that I enjoyed being able to advise clients, but I was not having the amount of direct interaction with the clients that I had hoped for.

The owner of the business at the time did not communicate with clients well. He was unable to simplify tax and accounting terms into plain language, so I was seeing clients leaving confused and frustrated. This upset me; as professionals, we were here to help our clients, and these individuals did not feel like they were being helped. To add insult to injury, they were given a bill for the advice they did not understand.

I had always planned on owning my own public accounting firm one day, and this was the firm that I had planned on purchasing. In my eyes, I was seeing a good firm slowly losing clients as they did not mesh with the owner. How the firm was being run was not consistent with my morals and my ethics.

I had to make a decision at that point—do I buy him out or find a new job? I knew I could get a different job nearby, but it would be an hour commute. My husband worked long days out of town in the wilderness logging, so he would not be available if there was a crisis with our young children (3 and 5 at the time) and if I took a different job, neither would I. Finding another job was not an option. I felt that I needed to buy the business and be around for our kids while doing what was right for the clients at the same time. I actually did not want to buy the business this soon as my kids were so young. But buying the business meant that I would be able to be true to my morals and ethics as well as be more available to them as I could juggle my responsibilities better.

How I became a CPA

I was bored working a minimum wage job in a very slow bar with a Bachelors degree in Animal Biology. I had wanted to be a veterinarian but the competition to get into one of the four colleges in Canada that offered the program was intense, and I was unsuccessful. I was complaining one day to my sister about the situation. Her reply was, "You like math, you like problem-solving, you are anal retentive – why don't you try bookkeeping or accounting?" So I looked into what those were, and it looked interesting.

The closest university college, University of the College of the Cariboo, (UCC) had a branch in my town. I looked at what they offered, and there was a program called an Accounting Technician Diploma Program. I had missed the deadline for the current year, but in the meantime, I could take some courses by correspondence. Add the correspondence courses to the semester's worth of credits from my previous degree, and I had almost finished the first year before even applying for the program.

When I had my interview to get into the program, I told them, "I have completed all but 2 of the courses from first year. Is it possible to take those courses and second year at the same time?" Being the proactive person that I am, anytime that I see an obstacle, I am generally climbing over it before anyone else realizes it is there. They accepted me into the second year of the program with no hesitation.

Halfway through my first semester, I figured out the difference between bookkeeping and accounting. Bookkeeping is looking at the trees; accounting is managing the forest. I didn't want to do just basic bookkeeping. I wanted to do more than that.

There were three different accounting designations in Canada at the time but only one was recognized internationally and, as I did not want to limit myself, I chose the Chartered Accountant designation. I figured out the prerequisites that I needed to get into the Chartered Accountant program and rearranged my second semester to fit them all in. I ended up with seven courses in the second semester and had to drop a class that I needed to get my diploma. I never did get the Accounting Technician Diploma; I am one course short. Instead, I had focused on the long-term goal of getting my CA designation instead of the short-term goal of getting a diploma that was no longer the right goal. My goals had changed.

I took all my courses, got my prerequisites, found a job with a public accounting firm, and jumped into the training courses to become a Chartered Accountant. Three and a half years later, I had passed all of the courses and I wrote my UFE, Uniform Final Exam, recognized as one of the hardest exams in the world. It was not fun but I passed and became a Chartered Accountant.

By that point, I had trained with a very renowned but very tough firm, where what I learned, I learned quickly, and I learned it well. And then, as I had finished up my designation, my husband and I decided to start a family.

What drives me to do what I do

I always saw my parents helping people, going beyond and doing what was needed to actually get the job done. Part of that is from growing up in a rural neighbourhood where neighbours helped neighbours. If I have the ability to help people, how can I not use it?

I feel grateful every time I can solve what appears to be an extremely difficult issue: when I see the worry go away from someone's eyes because someone else understands the issue and says they can help; when I can explain an accounting or tax issue in plain English or layman's terms so that my clients can make informed decisions because they understand; when I am able to have them toss the ball in my court, and I can toss it back to them with everything done, no worries.

I am a good problem solver, so I help people solve their business or tax problems. What is the issue? The real issue, not the window coverings that are masking what needs fixing or dealing with. What is the end goal and how do we get there? What needs to get done in order to fix this? The key is to break the problem down to its fundamentals and deal with them one by one.

Some days I just have to be a good listener and use some common sense to help deal with the problem. Other days, my knowledge of accounting or tax laws is what is needed. And some days you just need to tell people that yes, they do know what they are doing and they are on the right path. Keep on going.

The reaction from my family

My mom had sort of a mixed reaction when I told her and my dad that I wanted to buy the business. She was worried about the amount of work involved and how I was going to be able to manage it all because I had small kids and I wasn't quite ready. I had only been a CA for 5 years at that point and had never been the main accountant for any of the files in the office. But I had kept in contact with fellow CA students who were senior to me who I felt would be willing to help me out. And all of the staff in the office said that they were behind me if I purchased the firm.

On top of that, we had just purchased a 10-acre hobby farm 20 minutes out of town that has a 15 tree orchard. In addition, I was the main caregiver for our kids due to Ryan's very long hours at work. Running a business was going to really stretch me thin. But at the same time, she was very proud and pleased that her daughter thought she was capable of doing this. My dad felt the same way. "It's a big step and a gamble, but a good one."

Ryan, my husband's comment was "Cool. I'm a bit nervous, but it's a wise investment for the future," followed by quite a few late night conversations of, "Okay, go through this again. How much does my paycheque have to cover for all these loans and mortgages you're talking about?" Everyone was concerned but extremely supportive.

Adversity – Rural Living

I grew up as a latch-key kid: someone who at a young age (11 years old in my case) took the school bus home to an empty house. Depending on which schools we attended, my older sister came home at the same time or an hour later once she was in high school. We lived half an hour from town in a rural area on 10 acres.

Coming home to an empty house taught me a lot about myself. It also meant that I was responsible for a lot more than a kid in town was expected to do. That early responsibility helped to form my character and personal integrity.

My sister and I shared the chores: chopping and stocking firewood, tending to the animals, cooking dinner and anything else that Mom and Dad had asked us to do. We learned which of us was better at different chores and which chores went faster with both of us doing them. We could pick the order of the chores and when to do them as long as they were all done when Mom and Dad got home. Do the chores quickly and get more free time or watch the TV show and hope that we got the chores done before our parents arrived. Or could we fit the chores in when the commercials were on?

Our house was heated with a wood stove, so when we came home, the first thing to do was to get a fire going. That meant that we were also responsible for not burning the house down. This taught us to be mature and responsible enough to not take chances with the house that we lived in. Dad taught us the basics for how to start a fire but also showed us what to do in case of a chimney fire. We were not given this responsibility lightly. We were asked by Mom and Dad if we felt mature enough to be home by ourselves and if we were comfortable with the responsibility of starting a fire, feeding it and the possible consequences of a chimney fire.

I took pride in the ability to start a good fire that burned well and had the house warm quickly. It took trial and practise to find the best way to stack the wood, the amount of kindling and paper, and how far to damper the stove to get the fire going properly. If you turned the fan on at the top of the stairs, you would draw the hot air upstairs and get the heat circulating faster than if you did not. I got to the point that I could have our 2,000 sq ft house warm in half an hour on a winter's day.

Raising animals taught me to think of others before myself. My sister and I were in the 4-H program and raised a small herd of sheep. We also had a horse or two. Animals got fed and watered before you did because they were not able to do that on their own. We have the responsibility of taking care of them because we were the ones that domesticated them and made them dependent on us. An animal learns to trust you when you fix things for them and when you provide them with food and give them water. They also taught me about a work ethic and about patience. Whether you are sick or healthy, you still need to take care of your animals as they depend on you. Not feeding the animals is not an option. We sat down for dinner once, and Dad asked me if I had fed the animals as they were quite noisy outside. For some reason, I had not, and I told him so. He made me get up from the dinner table right then and there and go feed the animals. That made an impression on me and hammered home the lesson that those who are dependent on you come first.

I was a small child, so I had to learn different ways of doing tasks that required strength and to find tools that allowed me to do the jobs that I was given. In the winter, the animals' water buckets would freeze during the day, so after school when I needed to refill them, I first had to get the ice out of the buckets. I was not strong enough to hold the bucket up and slam it to the ground to break the ice up like Dad was. Instead, I would put the bucket on the ground upside down and hit it with a small sledge hammer, resulting in the ice breaking up and falling out. I learned the value of using brains instead of brawn to get the same result.

Living in a rural setting, I learned to be self-sufficient and independent as there was not always someone around to ask how to do things. I had to think and plan before doing something as there may not be anyone around if I screwed up or got hurt. Waiting was not always an option for getting something done, so I just had to figure it out by myself.

I learned what I was actually capable of. I was a determined (read: stubborn) child according to my Mother. I would figure out a way of doing things and getting things done even if people did not think that I was physically capable of doing it. Too short? Find a way to get to the height that you needed by standing on something, climbing something or by getting good at jumping. Not strong enough? Find a tool that will make it easier or figure out a different way to do it.

The early responsibility and the trust that my parents put in me gave me the self-confidence, independence and determination to be the person that I am now. Growing up as a latch-key kid in a rural setting on a hobby farm helped to make me the person that I am today.

How I juggled the business and my young family

In order to make it work, I had to be really good with time management and figure out how to get things done in a limited amount of time. With my husband Ryan working out of town so much, I was often on my own with our two young boys.

Ryan's family has always been there to help. His mom and dad have been the after school care providers for my kids since my eldest was in kindergarten. I have been able to rely on them for the sudden emergencies that always seem to come up when you have kids.

Finding a solution for childcare that worked for me was crucial so I could spend extra hours at the office. The other thing is I needed to be able to work from home if necessary. Having a computer station at home is important to me so you can work from home when the kids get sick or you get sick, and you can get something done when you're not in the office. Many a time, I put the kids to bed and then turn on the computer and do some work at home.

Unique challenges

My biggest challenge is that I don't reliably have a partner at home who can help me due to the industry he works in. This is especially strained during tax season, which happens to be March and April when spring break hits. My mom and dad live quite far away, so they don't get to see the kids very much. So ever since I bought the business, the kids have been going to my parents' for spring break. Then I can work long hours because the kids aren't home, and I don't have to worry about my husband. I can get up at 3:30 in the morning and I get to the office at 4:00 in the morning and I will work until 5:00 or 6:00pm. I work an entire week of crazy hours to get as far ahead as I can, so when the kids are back in town, I can be at home with them.

There are eight of us in the office; four of us have young children, and four don't. The staff without children help us out when we need to take time off. For example, at Christmas time, they have the office, and the four of us with kids are able to take two weeks off. I know my staff may not want to work overtime hours during our really busy season, so I hire extra staff instead. For the past three years, I've been bringing in a co-op student from my alma mater, Thompson River University, to help us with our busy season. They're the extra body that does the data entry, and extra work for us, so that the rest of us aren't putting in extremely crazy hours. Maybe a little more overtime, but not that much.

Managing staff

When I bought the business, all of the staff stayed and were just fine with me being their new boss. I had done sort of a query of, "What do you think of me buying the business?" None of them had issues with it and they were with me for most of the way. There were three staff plus myself: two of them are still working with me and the other gentleman retired. I'm now up to seven staff, plus myself, with a co-op student during tax season.

Sometimes it is amazing how much trust my staff put in me, but at the same time, it's reciprocal. I trust them to do what's best for the firm. They feel comfortable enough that if they don't know the answer, they say so. If you empower them with the trust and ability to make their own decisions that impact the firm, they will come through for you.

I had a friend who had a rant on Facebook not long ago that summed up how I hope I am treating my staff and how they are treating my business. He got a job at a heavy duty equipment shop where he ran inventory, shipping/receiving and accounts payable. He was nervous being responsible for approving cheques for hundreds of thousands of dollars a month and upon asking his boss, the owner, the 5th question of the day about yet another invoice he got told, "Why are you bugging me with this? If this was your business what would you do with this invoice? I trust you, keep up the good work and don't ask me this stuff, if there is a problem I'll let you know." This gave him a total sense of pride and empowerment he has never forgotten, and any job he has had since he has read the sign on the door as "Friend's name Inc ." Employers, give staff a chance, make them accountable, empower them, a compliment goes a long way, make a difference. Employees, step up, take pride in your work, it's your name on the door, so don't ruin it.

As I say to my staff, "The only reason that my name is on the door is that I had big enough balls to get this far into debt. Without you, that name is not on the door."

Growing my business

I am quite proud of where I have taken my firm in four years. I have doubled the number of staff which in turn means that I have doubled the work that the office does. When I bought the practice, the office had done 323 personal tax returns the prior year. In contrast, four years later we finished over 700 personal tax returns by the end of April. Additionally, many people who had not filed their taxes for several years came in after tax season to get caught up on prior years returns.

One of the other main things I did shortly after I bought the business was move to a new location. We were on the second story in the office building, and nobody knew we were there. We had no retail signage at all. The staircase to reach our office was dark and dreary, and kind of scary; the lights were never all fully working. The first thing I did, was move the office downstairs. The main floor happened to have an open spot that was absolutely perfect. It was a professional office before us, a financial advisor. We moved downstairs and put some signs on the door and posters in the window. Any time you pass by our window, there is always some sort of decoration in the window for something that's going on, be it Breast Cancer Awareness month with pink bras in the window, to Remembrance Day in November with poppies all over the window. We always have the office decorated somehow to show support for what is happening in the community.

Drawing on my internal resources

I have strength of character, courtesy of how my parents raised me. I recently had an email from a person that I legally could not talk to due to privacy laws as they were not the client but were associated to a file I was working on. She said, "You have a very reputable name in town for being by the book." To me that was the greatest compliment that I could ever have received.

When I am in a situation that I am not sure about, I ask myself what would my Dad or Mom do depending on what the situation I am in is. For example, my Dad was known in the Ministry of Forestry as the person to go to if you needed something done. Even if it was not in his area, he would get the right person on the job and make sure that if he had said it would be taken care of, that it was. Both Mom and Dad would do what was right no matter what people said about them. You don't just do the job, you do the job right.

Many a time I would remember Mom going up and down the aisles of the grocery store looking for something. Finally, she would ask me to go find someone and ask them where the item was. If you do not know, ask someone. This is the best advice that Mom ever taught me.

I learned that if you need to talk to someone, talk to someone. Don't bottle it up because the worst thing you can do is to not talk about the problems you're having. And if you don't know from your friends who you can talk to, maybe there another business owner or another group of people going through the same thing. I belonged to a group of women business owners who would meet once a month over drinks and cookies and we would complain about everything from our sons and their weird fixations to staff shortages in our businesses. Realizing that you are not the only one who has or is going through these issues makes you appreciate that there are solutions out there and people who can help you.

And if you are unable to take care of the situation yourself, there is no failure in that. Go ask for help instead of falling on your face trying to do it all. Most people love to be asked to help out because that is the best way to show your feelings for someone.

Drawing on my external resources

Having my family helping with the kids is such a huge support. I also do noontime yoga on Wednesdays. I value and enjoy my time with family, friends, and mentors. I try to get away and have time to myself. And this is the biggest one: it's important to have fun! Snowmobiling is what we love to do. There's nothing like going 122 MPH on a snowmobile. Find something that you can do to release stress. For instance, Martial Arts, like Taekwondo, is great because you can kick the living crap out of a punching bag. Doing something that is not related to your work is good as that can take enough of your concentration allowing you to relieve stress.

Find a similar type of business owner—and this is something I have done—find a mentor. They don't have to be in your town; they don't even have to be in your state or province. My mentor happens to be in Manitoba. Find a mentor that is willing, even if you have to pay money for it. Someone that you can e-mail, phone, anything along those lines, that is willing to be a sounding board for you. Find somebody that you can talk to, that you can vent to, who can hopefully help you come up with ideas. It is money well spent. Professionals are worth it - that's why they're professionals. They have the resources to be able to help you.

You have to recharge your mental batteries so that you can keep being the person that you want to be when life gets you down. One way to do that is to learn from other people. I keep going back to a taped lecture by John Rohn. His ideas and examples are simple and very straightforward but he has a subtle sense of humour that really gets his point across. Each time I listen, I pick up more ideas on how to keep motivated.

The importance of a positive mindset

If you lose that positive mindset, it's hard. I had to re-home my dog last summer at 10-and-a-half years old. It is very hard to find someone that is willing to take a senior dog and it completely destroyed any of my keeping it together, getting ahead, and being proactive instead of reactive in my business this summer.

I could tell by how my staff were acting, that without that firm direction on the rudder, you might really screw your business up if you don't have the mindset where it's supposed to be. I learned that this summer.

Our team does a yearly retreat. It's not physical team building. It's more mental: Where do we want to go? How do we want to get there? We had to do a lot of repair work at our team retreat this year because we had had a lot of personal tragedies and major upsets in the spring and summer that needed to be addressed. It really affected the morale at the office, especially with me grieving the loss of my dog and not providing clear direction and leadership for my team. So yes, a positive mindset is huge. Without that, "Yes, we can do it!" the best we're going to do is tread water and maybe sink. But at the same time, once you hit bottom, try it again. You never know. What you learned might be the best thing that happened to you and will help you to not do it again. Making mistakes is the best way to learn because you'll never make them again. And trust me, I've made some entertaining ones that I will never do again.

5 tips to choosing success over adversity

1. **Plan.** This is a big one. You still need to do. You can't be in the planning stages forever but if you jump right into the do without the planning, you don't know where you're going to end up. So plan but do, and revisit that plan over time, so you actually do remember where you're supposed to be going. It's sort of like the people who plug into their GPS but don't clue in that they're driving down a road that nobody has ever driven down and it's covered with 3 feet of snow. You might be getting in the right direction but you might not actually be on the right road.
2. **Take a risk.** If you don't try, you will never know if it's possible. I was honestly terrified and excited at the same time when I bought the practice. But at the same time, if I didn't, where would I be right now? I would have somebody else raising my children and me working for a mine that may or may not be shutting down in five years.

3. **Take time for yourself.** Prioritize activities that are completely unrelated to the job or business. You need to be selfish sometimes to keep yourself balanced.

4. **Ask for help.** The worst case scenario is they say no and you're no worse off than you were before. Best case scenario, you have someone who is going to help you.

5. **Only listen to people who are encouraging you.** Take the naysayers' advice as things to look out for, but that doesn't mean that you can't do what you want to do. They say it takes anywhere from six to 10 positive comments to make up for one negative remark. So that means that you need six people telling you to go for it compared to that one naysayer. Sometimes, the hard part is finding those six people who are telling you to go for it, that you can do it.

How buying a business made me stronger

It made me stronger because it made me realize I can't do it all. I have to be able to trust my team—and it is a team, it's not just people. We are a team that works together. I can give them a task to do and I have to trust them to do it. But it's reciprocal. They have to trust that the task they have given me also gets done, and that goes for everybody on the team. You have a strong team when everybody in the business is willing to provide constructive criticism to anyone on the team, regardless of position. When I am being neurotic and stressing about minor issues, my team can tell me to relax and go away. It's an environment of respect, and there's not a hierarchy.

What I have learned

I have learned to keep thinking outside the box. I have always been like that. When I was a child, my dad gave my older sister and me a chore to do and it involved moving fence rails all the way over to where we were building a fence. But I really wanted to go for a horseback ride. I didn't want to do the chore I was given, so I came up with a solution to it that meant I could do both. I saddled up the horse and tied together about 20 logs, hooked it to the horse's saddle, and got him to do the work. I told my sister, "You spread them out, and I'll bring them over." When my dad came home, Kathleen was reading a book and I was gone. He said, "I gave you a chore to do," and Kathleen replied, "Yeah, it's done." He asked, "What do you mean it's done?" He figured it would take us 3 days but we managed to get it done in hours and I was happy because I got my horseback ride.

That's an example of thinking outside the box. What is it you want to do? Don't take things thrown in your path—yeah, they're obstacles, but you can get over them, or under them, or through them somehow. You just have to figure out how.

When you are going through a challenging time

Remember that you can do it. Stick to it. Look for a mentor, someone you can talk to. If you have a professional organization, a lot of them have counsellors you can talk to. They have websites that you can go to for information. Google it. You would be surprised how many things there are for that.

Think positive and when you're having one of those weeks that are all Mondays, go take some time for yourself. Step back, look at it, get back out of the situation and think, "How will this impact me in the future? Is it really that important or am I just making it important because it's right in my face?" Take that time to step back, think about it. Take that time to yourself, put yourself back on that even keel, and then get right back at it again.

And it might be that the thing you're not doing right now is what you should be doing. Not the other one that you're freaking out over. But above all have fun. Nothing is so bad that you can't laugh at yourself.

About the Author, Carrie Ware, CPA, CA.

Carrie Ware & Company, Inc.
Merritt, BC
www.carrieware.ca
Phone: 250-378-2215

Carrie Ware is a Chartered Professional Accountant in public practice in Merritt, BC, Canada. She owns her own Chartered Professional Accountant firm and is a leader in her community. She is a strong and capable person who can take a difficult problem, break it down into easily understood issues, and help solve it. Carrie is a lifesaver for her clients because she is always there to help them and support them in making their businesses more successful.

Carrie lives on a 10 acre hobby farm with her husband Ryan and two young boys. Between giving people business advice or preparing taxes, she can be found looking for eggs hidden by free range chickens, riding quads or snowmobiles with the family or drag racing

CARRIE WARE, CPA, CA.

at 120 MPH on a snowmobile. Alternatively, she may be curled up in a chair reading a good book or crocheting an afghan or out weeding in the garden.

93

Overcoming Obstacles

By Colleen Preston

I made the decision to become an entrepreneur over 20 years ago in order to have the opportunity to be home to raise my two children by myself. I was a computer instructor and writer for Microsoft Certification manuals. My current business is a private training studio called Oasis Training that provides specialized fitness training, personal development, nutrition and workshops on health and lifestyle.

I work mainly with people over 40 who want more from life whether it is physically, emotionally, and/or financially. Many people come to me in search of motivation, direction, goals, or plans for improving their life. I help solve various issues from understanding physical issues with aging, injury recovery/prevention, weight management, sports goals to creating strategies for success. I try very hard to make everything motivating, exhilarating and enjoyable.

I am passionate about helping others and watching them grow and enjoy their lives. I want to give back everything I didn't get. Dignity, Healing and Support. As a child, I spent summers on Mayne Island, BC where we didn't have TV, phones or a radio. We spent most of our days exercising and reading. I also spent a lot of time cooking healthy meals. Although our lifestyle sounds healthy, it was an extremely stressful home. I found exercise became my way of escaping anxiety from the anger and hatred that my mother had for me. I also watched as my mother and sister became obsessed with fitness training and had eating disorders. I desperately wanted to be different and find balance in my life somehow.

Many times in my life when things were extremely tough, there was no support. I would also withdraw and not tell my friends and extended family how bad things were. One of the books that I read which was very helpful was The Four Agreements. I've read it about 10 times to grasp what it was saying about being authentic and true to yourself. I wanted so badly to become fully authentic and be able to have boundaries without worrying that people wouldn't like me. I would say that becoming authentic and helping others to do so as well has been an incredible influence in my later life. Creating and facilitating a workshop called The Vines That Bind Us and currently working on completing the full book to go with it is very exciting now.

At 23, I was one of very few female computer instructors, so I had to prove myself. I was young so how could I know anything? Also, being female, I had to work harder. In 1996 I had a terrible fall off of a horse and broke my left wrist, injured my shoulder and elbow and was told I might never type again. That was the end of my career writing training manuals and teaching computers. Before I had the chance to recover from my broken wrist, I found myself in a nasty divorce with two small children in diapers while in yet another cast after more surgeries. Strangely, the rehab for my arm, re-ignited my interest in physiology and fitness. As I proceeded to rehabilitate myself, I began my education in physiology and fitness with a thought to teach fitness instead of computers. Even though I never saw my parents and sister again, I was still intimidated to get into fitness.

A couple of my friends thought it was crazy to be a single mom opening a gym alone when I could have had a corporate position with my computer and writing skills, however, my friends have always known to just let me go and watched me run.

Often, successful women either make a choice that they are going to be a warrior or they are going to be a victim. I chose to be a warrior.

When I first decided to open a studio and continue writing I was doing quite well. I was single and dating on occasion. In 2006, a well-known public figure, the Mayor of my city and also my boss, asked me on a date. I thought it was strange, but I agreed. The first date was a disaster as he took me to a public event where I knew everyone. I think he was used to getting all of the attention, so I am not sure if it made him angry or intrigued... Being around him gave me a very bad feeling in my stomach, and I told him I didn't want to see him again. Also, I was just starting a new business, and when you have two children to support, it is not a good idea to be distracted.

No matter how I tried to tell this man that I would be a friend to him, he refused to accept that I wasn't interested and he started stalking my family and me. He told me that no one says no to him especially because he was the Mayor. He spent the next 10 months terrorizing me and my two young children (10 and 12 years old) by following me around, hiding outside my classes, attending my home uninvited, hiding at the parks I would be teaching at, waiting at my work, screaming death threats on the phone and breaking into my home and then bizarrely calling me back right away to ask me to go for coffee. He would barge into my home after school when I was teaching and tell my son because he was the Mayor, he had the right to be in my house opening my mail and going through all of my belongings. I continually begged him to stop because I didn't want to involve the police and then the whole town. Nothing worked. He wouldn't stop. I dreaded the day I had to report him because the second that I did, my private life would become public and I would have an even more difficult task of running a small business alone than I was already facing with the harassment.

Trying to pretend that nothing was wrong in front of my clients was difficult. The harassment escalated to the point I knew I would be dead either way, so I finally called 911. That call was the beginning of a very long and stressful time for me. Jail, court and restraining orders did nothing to stop the harassment. It was hard to pretend I was okay and continue to run a "positive, motivating" business to help other people.

The evening that I called 911, this unstable man had broken into my gym, completely obliterated from either drugs or alcohol or both. He was frothing at the mouth, shouting profanities that didn't make sense, kicking my friend in the ribs as he was doing ab exercises. He had brought rope and duct tape with him to hang me. It was frightening. That was the beginning of a living hell for me for years.

After that horrible night, my life became public. I was inundated with reporters, phone calls and even hate mail. The City whom I was contracted to work for knew the "Mayor" had a restraining order but ignored it and told him of my whereabouts. This insane man breached his restraining order three times with no consequence. Crown Counsel strongly instructed me that I was not to talk to anyone or tell my side of the story because of the upcoming court case. Me and my family were invisible to everyone. To this day, my story has never been told, and the minor charges he received were nothing to stop him from continuing to be a predator.

For many months, I would train a client and go back to bed between clients. It was better for me to be sleeping than awake in the nightmare I was living. I didn't open my mail; I barely collected money. I almost lost my house and my gym. I was sick to my stomach every day. I was destroyed inside and had to hide my feelings. And then, when I was at a very weak moment one day, I left my parents a message. As expected, they didn't call back or care. It tortured me even though I knew they wouldn't call me back. My sister asked a friend what was going on and when he told her to ask me herself she promptly and coldly stated, "Oh well, it was only morbid curiosity anyway".

One day, I decided that if I was going to survive the trauma and public humiliation, I needed to get up and do something that scared me even more than having my life threatened. So I opened a commercial location for my gym. I thought, *I have had this happen before in a sense when my mother told me she should have killed me, and I lived through that.* That thought made me angry enough that I decided to repeat to myself, *You're not going to take me out, I am not going down.* No one can know what it is like to be hated, ignored by the Justice system and live in hell on earth unless they have been there.

The day that I opened the new location, I had no idea that it happened to be International Women's Day so I thought it was a good sign. Unfortunately, timing is everything. The commercial location opened in March of 2008, and soon after, the market crashed which meant for many of my clients that the first thing they stop is their personal training.

A few months after the business opened, the court case came up for a decision, and I was brought right back into the hell of not being heard, of listening to lies and the injustice. He laughed at me at court because knew he would get away with it. The "Mayor" is the boss of the Chief of Police; the "Mayor" has more pull than some single mother struggling with no family. I had actually been awaiting the court appearance because it was finally the opportunity for my children and myself to read out our testimony but we did not get to. That was so incredibly disheartening. People were outraged. He refused to step down as Mayor and a group of community members even had signs and marched around the City Hall. I had an amazing client that stood up at Council meetings, demanding he step down. He did not care. It was insanity. After the court gave him four minor charges, he was set free with a restraining order. I was financially devastated and emotionally weak, but I had to keep working through it to support my children.

By 2010, I was recovering financially. One day after golfing, I met someone that asked me to go for dinner. On the second date, he kept asking questions about my case with the Mayor. I had no idea how he remembered me on the news 2 years prior. It was very unnerving and brought me back to feeling insecure. I thought I was being ridiculous or paranoid and since I hadn't dated for years, I second-guessed myself.

My lack of boundaries, confidence, fear of men and standing up for myself put me in a position where I was attacked by this man at his house. He locked me in his room with three dogs barking and crying and scratching at the door as he beat my face, slammed my head on a ceramic floor for 45 minutes and boxed my ears. He strangled me and hung me by my jaw. I fell unconscious a few times. He never spoke. It was like he was a robot performing a mundane job. The only words he said were my name when he was slapping my face to wake me up when I was unconscious. When he was strangling me, my feet were not touching the ground, and I felt like I was shaking uncontrollably, but I was actually looking down at myself from above. I thought, "I am going to die, that's me hanging there." Just before I couldn't breathe anymore, he let go, and I fell to the ground. I started praying out loud that if there was a God, and if I could see my children again, I would do whatever God would tell me to do. I would do whatever he says. It was unbelievable; suddenly the attack stopped, he looked at his watch and actually phoned the police on himself. It was very strange. He left the room to call the police, and I scrambled for my phone. Before I could pick myself up and run, he returned. He said, "You're not going anywhere." He looked at his watch and said, "I've got time before the cops come." After hitting me a few more times and boxing my ears, he yelled profanities at me and told me to get out. I ran screaming out of the house to the police car. As I sat in the car, I saw him at the door. He had changed his clothes and was all dressed up, and acted like nothing happened. I couldn't talk properly because my lips were so swollen so the police just thought I was some hysterical woman. It was devastating, and I don't know if I will ever fully physically or emotionally recover from that. I had a concussion so severe that I couldn't exercise and teach the way I used to. I couldn't balance, I had vertigo, I still faint all of the time to this day, and I just couldn't live in my hometown anymore.

Incredibly, I still had a business to run and went to work with bruises everywhere. I had two children to care for in a debilitated state – again. It was terrible for them to see me so badly beaten all over my face, ears, mouth. My teeth were turning black and falling out. I agonized over what to do. After deliberating and trying to cope, I had a contractor client who offered to renovate my house to move the gym back home, but his real agenda was that he thought I was getting a settlement for my face. He pushed me to sign a form when I was still on pain medication, with vertigo and fainting. I found out a month later that the form actually said I would owe him $23,000.00 for a renovation that he told me would be bartered – for training. Again, I had to go to court and fight! I was done. I was just done. So many predators. I was exhausted, traumatized and completely lost and alone. I had to decide to close everything down and leave. I had to give up.

All of those years of my life, up to 44 years old, I had lived in a town close to my parents, hoping one day they would talk to me, that they would see me as a valuable community member, successful, and then maybe they wouldn't hate me. Now I was a failure. I think I believed my mother that I should be dead and there it is, two people tried to kill me.

In July of 2012, I closed all 3 locations of my business, gave most of my belongings away and left town. I travelled, I wrote, and I took on random jobs for a year. I had to decide what I wanted in my life, so I wrote everything out. I wrote my workshop The Vines That Bind Us, and I used it on myself. I needed to find my Oasis. I wrote workshops, I purged, I learned, I cried, I attended various styles of counselling. Then in September of 2013 when I came back to BC, suddenly there it was. I found my oasis and began to rebuild.

I promptly cut the ties to my hometown and let go of my need to reconcile with my parents. I sold my house and bought a place in my oasis where I spend a lot of time training amazing people, writing, reading and making brand new, very special friends. I provide dignity, healing and support and hold my workshops to help others and live each day, saying YES to as many interesting opportunities as possible. In my first year of business, I travelled to the Middle East and Asia and have sent my children to Rome! I am not saying no to anything wonderful again.

What got me through the tough times were my faith, my extended family and my children. I rely on my personal competitiveness and courage. My love of fitness and sports, eating well, nutrition, and the amazing real friends I have all contribute to staying strong. I enjoy much deeper relationships now. I found strength in finally creating and keeping boundaries. I found strength in being farther away from my parents. I believe that most of all, my children, my faith, my aunt, my grandmother and family in Winnipeg are what have always kept me from giving up. Seeing life on the positive side and having a sense of humour has always helped me cope.

I believe a positive mindset is the most powerful way to overcome adversity. If I encounter tough times, I know that times may be even tougher for someone else. I love sitting on the ocean in a kayak staring out at how huge the ocean is. It is humbling.

I believe it is vital to protect your mind with good thoughts. If you don't protect your mind, your thoughts will manifest negative results including creating sickness in your body as well as attracting more negativity. So why not try to keep the fresh air, fresh food and fresh ideas flowing?

5 tips to choosing success over adversity

1.) Truly believe in something
2.) Surround yourself in positivity (remove negativity)
3.) Educate yourself as much as possible
4.) Take responsibility for your life and forgive yourself
5.) Make a plan and be accountable

The events that I endured made me stronger because I realized the great desire I have to live. I still feel like I was given a second chance at life and it stopped me in my tracks. I don't take anything for granted. I also don't feel like I absolutely have to have my mother and father's acceptance, in fact I am going to go boldly forward to find out what they are hiding and not worry about what that truth might be.

All of these events changed me from being wild and quick to jump into things and not having boundaries. I consciously try to think things through and surround myself with what is good and healthy.

The moment I finished asking if there was a God that would let me live, I realized then that I needed to allow myself give love to other people and to accept love back. God spoke that night. "Go, love and be loved and walk away from hate."

I know for sure you really can create a beautiful, meaningful and abundant vision for yourself. I am living it now with my Oasis.

Believe that there is more in this world than what is in our heads and in our small space that we live. Be really clear about what you want and then go explore, learn, express yourself, and enjoy truth and success.

About the Author, Colleen Preston

Trainer/Speaker/Writer
Oasis Training
Email: info@oasistraining.ca
Website: www.oasistraining.ca
Facebook: oasistrainingcp
LinkedIn: colleenpreston
Phone: 604.993.1888

Colleen has been a successful entrepreneur for over 20 years. She started in the computer industry in 1989 as a writer for Microsoft Certification training manuals and taught computers all over BC and Nunavut. In 2003 she opened her first Private Personal Training Studio and grew the business to 10 trainers and 3 locations.

In 2015, she moved to the Sunshine Coast and is the owner of Oasis Training where she provides specialized personal training, exercise nutrition and personal development workshops. She enjoys working with people who are seeking motivation, success strategies and change.

With a diverse set of skills, Colleen develops all of her own material for workshops and marketing for her company. She also provides various writing, bookkeeping and business services for other companies.

She has several books awaiting publishing including a children's illustrated book series, The Vines That Bind Us personal development book and her personal story.

Finding the Gifts in Our Adversities

By Marsha Vanwynsberghe

Marsha Vanwynsberghe had a very challenging path with twists and turns that no one could have foreseen. A path that she did not plan on and would never knowingly choose. After years of hiding her struggles from the world and after a very painful period of personal growth, she decided her story had to serve a purpose. Marsha chose to publicly own her story by sharing it with others through speaking engagements, workshops, her blog and eventually her own booked called, "When She Stopped Asking Why"... A Mother's Journey Through Teen Substance Abuse and the Loving Path to Finding Her Clarity, Courage and Purpose.

Marsha shares her story as a mother who experienced teen substance abuse at a level far beyond experimentation. She decided to own her story and in the process found thousands of other families who were also impacted by teen substance abuse. In sharing her story she truly found her purpose to coach, teach and motivate other parents to let go of their shame, find their voice, release their guilt and own their own life again. Marsha is driven to connect with and inspire parents to stop owning the choices of their children and to take full responsibility for their own lives.

Marsha's story is for all the Moms who lost themselves while raising their kids, to all the parents who've struggled with their children and with themselves and to anyone else who is hiding from the world because their shame is driving the wheel. No matter what adversity you are fighting your way through, no matter what you are resisting, no matter how much pain you have experienced, the tools that

Marsha shares will assist you in taking control of your life and learning the power of surrender. That is where true, lasting change occurs.

I am honoured to share my story with you. I want you to know that you are never alone in your suffering. My wish is that my story will spark something in you. A spark of hope, a light, a glimmer of belief, or a complete shift in your mindset. You are capable of more than you realize. You are here for a reason, you have unique gifts, and you have a purpose that is yours to use to impact others.

I didn't always embrace this mindset and message. There were a number of years that I hated where my life was at; I hated God for giving me this life, which led me to hate myself for such terrible thoughts. I resented the fact that everyone else seemed to have what I wanted….a happy family with healthy kids and minimal challenges. At least it appeared that way from the outside, that is the trap of living a life in comparison of others. I did not ask for drugs to enter our life and when it did, I did everything humanly possible to stop it. It never stopped. It simply grew like a monster impacting all areas of our life.

A critical piece of the story is that I dedicated my entire life and career to working as a health and fitness expert. I spent 25 years working with people to help them make physical, emotional and transformational changes in their life. How could I possibly do that and have such a mess in my own personal life? I felt like such a hypocrite. It took every ounce of energy I had to "fake" my happiness in my life while I was with my clients. They didn't come to see me to hear complaints and stories of drama. My emotions were out of control by this point, and when I spoke of our story, I would break down in tears. I wasn't ready to share yet, not even close. At this point in my life, I was owning everyone else's actions, and tearing myself apart for not having the answers to fix it. It was a vicious circle that I couldn't break.

I wanted to hide our story, thinking the "phase" would eventually pass. I am not proud of my thought patterns and how I did or didn't handle it. I think I reacted the way that I did because shame and embarrassment were controlling my life. I was far more obsessed with the judgment of others than I ever thought I would be. I also recognize that these concerns did nothing to fix our situation. It was a massive waste of energy that I didn't have.

Drugs entered our household when our boys were only 12 and 13 years old. I was very sick at this time with a blood staph infection after years of repeated surgeries. This is when we found marijuana for the first time. It likely isn't the first time it was used, just the first time it was found. I have no doubt that we made many mistakes along the way, but I can say that I was always clear that it was not ok for them to use drugs and definitely not to be found in our house. My message never swayed, no matter how many times we found it.

During these early years, I felt like I was living a double life because we didn't share what was going on with our friends or family until almost two years later. It was out of pure shame that we hid – we were ashamed because we were upset about the frequent drug use, and embarrassed at our inability as parents to stop it. That is just where my mindset was at during this point in my life. As a society, we equate a child's behaviour to how well a parent does their job. It's a universal "unspoken" law. When we see a child throw a temper tantrum, the first thing we do is look at the parents. Or when a child is well behaved because they sit still, we think the parents did a great job of raising their kids.

Eventually, the drugs grew from marijuana use to other drugs such as meth, ecstasy and many other drugs that we didn't know about. Drugs impacted every single aspect of all of our lives.

How did it get to this stage? There were so many factors that contributed to the control that drugs had over our boys. At this point in our story, the boys' lives were completely changing who they were as people. That was one of the toughest things to watch as a parent. As it escalated, they would be missing for days and sometimes weeks at a time. When they were home, we were constantly fighting and removing drugs from the home. The police became regular visitors in our home. Eventually, the boys stopped going to school altogether. We removed all extra privileges including sports, phones, and eventually living arrangements. I don't expect everyone to understand the decisions we had to make. I do want to share that we did everything humanly possible to stop this cycle of drugs and what it was doing to our family.

All we were told was that "everyone's hands were tied because they were minors." The most common advice we were given was to pray that we make it until they were 18 years old. The Young Offenders Act in Canada meant that kids between the ages of 12 - 16 were given multiple chances with minimal to no consequences. No one had any solutions or suggestions, and no one had any control over them. Our boys were truly untouchable, and they knew it. It was impossible to convince kids to try and change something when there's no repercussions, consequences or reason to change.

For the first 2 - 3 years of our 6-year journey to today, I hid from the world because I honestly couldn't believe what was happening. It was ridiculous to hide because it wasn't a secret from anyone. Everyone knew that something was going on with our family, yet no one knew how critical things had become. In all honesty, I was the one that wasn't ready to face how big of a demon it had become.

I knew something had to change. I started reading personal development books, listening to guided meditations, YouTube videos, podcasts, anything positive and motivational to shift my mindset. I stumbled across Brene Brown's books and her Ted Talk on Vulnerability. Her message hit me as though she was speaking directly to me. I started to come to grips with owning my own story. It was real. There was no hiding from it any longer. In fact, the longer I hid from it, the more it controlled me, and the more power it had over me. I didn't realize I was the one that was giving it so much power. My story was dictating every single aspect of my life to the point that I was no longer freely living my own life. I was intrigued by the concept of owning my own story and what that meant.

My interpretation of owning my own story means coming to a place where I can understand what my role is in the situation and what someone else's role is in the situation. In other words, learning how to own everything that is mine to own. That includes: my behaviour, my reaction, my attitude, my mindset in how I handle and react to everything that occurs around me. In owning my own story, I clearly understood what part was my story and what wasn't mine to own.

This was a critical first step. I believe it's important to own my own story, no matter what the story, because it means taking responsibility for my own life and taking ownership for how I choose to live it and what I do with it. I believe that it is allowing me to be in a place of not blaming somebody else for where my life is at and ultimately taking responsibility for what I can control.

Even though I started to understand the importance of owning my story, I couldn't figure out how I could possibly share it with others. Everyone would obviously blame us for the problems in our family because subconsciously I couldn't help but still blame myself. A mom is supposed to keep her kids safe, protect them from harm, and guide them into adulthood with a life full of potential opportunities. I felt like such a failure as a mom, a wife and a human being.

When I decided to publicly own my story and not theirs, I received so many messages from strangers thanking me for being so open as it showed them that they were not alone. I was featured on CBC morning radio, I spoke at multiple events and on many MoMonday's stages. I started a blog, created live videos and a podcast called "Own Your Choices, Own Your Life." Eventually, it resulted in my own book being released in the fall of 2017. The more I stepped out and shared my story, the more I received the messages of confirmation that I knew I had to continue on this path.

Not everyone understood this journey that I was on. In fact, for many prior generations we generally lived with the mindset that we don't share our problems or our secrets with the world. Personally, I believe that this approach of hiding doesn't serve any of us. I knew that something had to change and I started to believe that this was my purpose in this whole mess. Once I could see the light and a purpose, I continued to live with faith and follow its path.

In order to create a change in our lives, I had to stop trying to fix everyone else. I was spending every ounce of energy on things that I had zero control over and absolutely no energy on the things that I could control, which was me. Creating change required a complete overhaul on the priorities in my life. I took a hard look at my values, my personal boundaries (I didn't have any), and took control over my own life and truly surrendered everything else. My inner circle of friends transformed as many friends disappeared or walked away. I have no ill feelings about that as no one knew how to handle our situation. It took me years to learn, so I had no business being angry at others for not knowing what to say or do. Changing my life required that I completely change. It was the only way.

One of the biggest barriers to owning my story was overcoming the judgment of others. I was far more concerned with this than I like to admit. This stemmed from the fact that I felt like I had failed as a parent, and this change in mindset was one of the last things I had to let go of. When I had the ah-ha moment that no one could judge me harder than I had judged myself, my entire thought process shifted. Once this happened, the judgment piece became literally non-existent and that in of itself was the most freeing feeling in the world.

It feels as though it took years to see the light and at the same time it happened in an instant. At one point in our journey, I was curled up in a ball on the floor, endlessly crying, begging for solutions and trying to find the energy to stand up again. I heard a voice that said, "Stop". I know this may sound crazy to some people, but the voice was crystal clear. *I kept hearing the word STOP!!*

At this point, we were on the verge of losing both of our boys to either an overdose or suicide and both instances potentially happening in our own home. No matter how hard I tried to stop it, we were at this point. When I heard the voice say Stop, I understood it to say stop trying to control, fix and manage the situation. It was time to let go. I resisted this for so long because my original interpretation of surrender meant quitting, and I was not a quitter. I was completely wrong in the definition of the word. Surrender was what I resisted the most, and it was exactly what I had to do. I couldn't own their choices and expect them to own them at the same time. If any change was going to occur, they had to be the one to own their choices and the consequences of their choices. That was truly the turning point of my story.

Learning to surrender and own what was mine became a daily ritual that took a lot of practice to embrace. Over time I realized that I had to create a list of non-negotiables that I needed to do daily if I was going to handle our situation. I couldn't be frustrated with my ability to handle our situation and at the same time do absolutely nothing to improve my chances of handling what we had been given. I was up to me, and I was the only one who could make the choices I needed to make. I couldn't blame this on anyone else anymore. My priorities included owning my boundaries, prioritizing my health, exercise and fitness, mindset, a daily gratitude practice, and listening to my intuition. I became diligent in who I chose to spend my time with. If it was a person who was taking energy from me, being judgmental or controlling, I chose not to spend my time with them. It wasn't personal; I simply had to guard my energy like it was gold because it truly was. My tribe then and now is a massive contributing factor to bringing me to this point in my life. That is the piece that so many people miss. We aren't meant to face our challenges in life alone, and we won't find the answers on our own.

These activities became part of my daily practice, but it truly all started from my mindset. I had to believe that I was worthy of living a life full of happiness and joy, one that I controlled. Mindset was everything. Through my reading and work, I understood that my thoughts controlled my beliefs and the actions that I did or did not take. It all started with my mindset, and my mindset was up to me to control and manage. I was embracing the importance and necessity of this step.

Repeating this process, day in and out, resulted in massive changes in my life. I felt stronger, more confident, in control and was living with a newfound degree of courage. I started to believe in myself again, and I started honouring my voice and my message. I reframed my thinking and called our adversities a gift. What a strange word to call the worst experience of my life.

I stumbled onto this word by accident. I started journaling and writing to sort through my thoughts. It took me so long to try to make sense of our life. Writing helped with the process. I was making progress and moving forward, yet a big part of me was still stuck.

I'm a very logical and analytical person, almost to a fault. I kept feeling as though there had to be a reason for why our family was in this experience. Every time I asked the question, I found myself stuck in the "why" question again. I knew that wasn't changing anything and it definitely wasn't productive. It was a constant game of tug of war. Then one day while I was writing, I realized that through this experience, I had finally found myself again. I found my strength, my courage, and my purpose. Ironically in the worst experience of my life is where I found myself again. I consciously started to call it a gift, because that would shift my anger and frustration. It would literally change my mindset and energy. If it truly was a gift, then I was meant to do something with it. It wasn't mine to keep to myself. It was mine to share with others, especially if I could use it to help others during the painful experiences in their life. The term gifts started to take on a life form of its own, and in that form, it started to show me a much bigger picture which involved helping and impacting others.

Our gifts actually aren't for us. Our gifts are meant to be shared with and used to impact the lives of others. Paying it forward in some way shape or form, became a new purpose. This was the birthplace of my speaking engagements and writing, and it gave meaning to a much bigger picture and purpose.

These lessons aren't just for me. They are for me to share with others to help ease their path and their struggles. That is my purpose, and I will continue to embrace it and be open to where it takes me in my life. Watching my clients progress, gain their confidence and create shifts in their life gives me fuel every single day.

To some, it appeared that I had everything in order, that I was positive and always able to handle the adversities our family was experiencing. I didn't just fall into this space; I crawled to get here. I crawled in the smallest baby steps, and I crawled through some of the ugliest and darkest days of my life. I was committed to my life. I wanted more for my life than where I was at. I worked through those lessons every single day in order to get to this point, the point where I could finally share my lessons with others. Even though those lessons were tied to some of the most painful experiences of my life, living through them was a critical experience and part of my survival.

As a result of drugs entering our lives, I completely changed as a person, and I learned to be grateful for the journey. Learning to let go of control of everyone else and taking control of myself completely changed my life. Everything stemmed from my relationship with myself. I could not fully love and have compassion for myself and hate all of the experiences in my life. Those experiences played a massive role in who I am today.

My advice to others going through a challenging time is to remind you that you are not alone and to reach out for support from others. If you do not have the people in your life to support you reach out further and find them. Someone somewhere is fighting the same battle as you, and they are praying for a solution and support because they're tired of battling their story alone. Allow yourself to be vulnerable and open. When you remove the people that aren't serving you and create space in your life, the most amazing people have room to come into your life. That is how change happens, by creating space and believing that you are worthy of the change because you absolutely deserve more in your life.

My final message, from a place of love, is that you know the answers. You might not always love the answers, but you do know what they are. Trust yourself and follow through. Pay attention to the cues your body and your energy are giving you. They are working to guide you in the right direction. You aren't here to fix everything, and in fact, you can only control yourself. Your actions, your reactions and your decisions are yours to own. When you create your non-negotiables, understand your values and embrace your boundaries, you will be in a position to make the necessary decisions to create change in your life. Listen to and respect yourself and live your life in integrity. Trust yourself as you've always known the answers. Your voice and your story matters. Someone, somewhere, is praying for you to find the courage to speak up and share your story.

About the Author, Marsha Vanswynberghe

Website: www.marshavanw.com
Email: marsha@marshavanw.com
Phone: 519.502.8425
Facebook: http://facebook.com /marshavanwynsberghe

For 25 years Marsha Vanwynsberghe has worked as a Kinesiologist and Personal Trainer. She coaches and mentors people to make physical changes in their bodies and emotional transformations in their lives.

Due to her life altering family crises, Marsha learned through first hand experience the power of personal growth, boundaries and values, expanding mindset, consistent exercise and clean nutrition. Many situations occur that are not part of our life plan and no one plans on adversities such as substance abuse issues in their family.

Marsha found her passion and purpose to inspire and assist others to find their voice and create change in their lives. She coaches people to learn the tools to live a life unstuck. She found the gifts in her adversities and now speaks openly on issues that no one wants to discuss.

Marsha is sharing her lessons learned and her story through coaching clients, speaking and her new workshop called "The Inspired Life Project." She is also a featured author in the book titled, "Influence", by Gerry Visca, as well as a co-author of the book Shine: Inspirational Stories of Choosing Success Over Adversity (Volume 2). Marsha is also the author of her first book called, "When She Stopped Asking Why…A Mother's Journey Through Teen Substance Abuse and the Loving Path to Finding her Clarity, Courage and Purpose.

Marsha lives in Waterloo, Ontario with her husband Brad. She has two sons. She loves to travel and is on a mission to share these lessons to help others live more fulfilled and impactful lives.

Connect with Marsha at www.marshavanw.com for a FREE 30 minute strategy session.

Mind Over Finances

By Michele Devlin

F rom all appearances, particularly on social media, I have a successful life, and it looks like it was easy to come by. My husband, Steve, and I have been married for 17 years. Our jocular teenage son is a blessing every day and our over-friendly and rambunctious border terrier, Ted, rounds out our little family. In a few weeks, we are off to travel through France and Italy and make a point of getting away every 3 to 4 months—preferably to a warm, sunny location because I crave it! We have an idyllic life on the Sunshine Coast and in Vancouver, with homes by the ocean in both areas. I am the CEO of two successful financial companies that I co-own with Steve.

I've written before. I started as a junior reporter while in college. During my time collecting classes at university as a professional student, I managed to beat out master and doctorate students for a job with a world-renown Economist, which ultimately led to being published in his book. Recently I co-authored the Amazon best-selling book *Simple Success Strategies for Women Entrepreneurs*. Not bad for the kid was told not to go to college, let alone university—because she was "too stupid" to go.

I wasn't stupid, just dyslexic. A trait I passed on to my son, who has an affinity for science and fortunately attends a school that recognizes he just learns differently than the status quo. And, thank goodness for Google! It gave me the crucial resource every Dyslexic person needs, an on-demand resource centre so I could look up the word quo because my spell checker couldn't figure it out either!

I wasn't as lucky to have the education my son is now getting, but I did figure out how I learned and that realization opened up my world to possibilities I thought were beyond the reach of this poor kid from Surrey. In adulthood, I had control over my destiny. I had control how I learned. I had control where I learned, and I had control of what I wanted to learn. Education gave me confidence in myself that I knew I had but sometimes didn't let shine through. It was my foundation; it held my values, it was the rock I could go back to-- even if only for a visit in my mind.

Our businesses are a reflection of our values and our life choices. That foundation I received in university is something I carry with me in all that I do. Start with building the foundation, creating the infrastructure to hold the concrete that is so malleable upon pouring and so strong when it finds its place, fills in the cracks and turning into the pedestal of strength to hold the living space we call home. Because if we think about living space, it's more than an actual house or other dwelling unit, living space is creating the life we want to have.

Why I do what I do

I love the pursuit of knowledge and education. I am a researcher by nature; I spent quite a few years in university, and I often feel uncomfortable if I don't know something. I love to learn. Even when faced with the daunting news of stage 3b colorectal cancer, I had to learn about my affliction, what was entailed in treatment and how to recover. So, when I come across people going through something that I have information or the knowledge on how to get it, I typically jump in and offer whatever help I can give them. If I can make someone's life easier, I will try. I've been in that place, and I'd rather not see people sitting there any longer than they need to. People came to me too in my time of need, to make things easier for me and that's what life is about. We're not here just to carry on our own individual lives. It will rapidly become a very lonely world if all we are concerned about is ourselves and even lonelier when we need help and there is no one to give it.

We all go through really tough times. If people don't get help or the resources they need, they end up in a place where depression or anxiety can set in. The world doesn't become a better place with the world not sharing. I hope I come across that way, that I'm caring and I want to help people. I want people to feel secure, to feel loved, and to feel their worth.

I can remember when I was a kid always looking for the fairness in life's situations. I really didn't like it when things weren't fair. Some people would attribute that to being a Libra. Maybe, but I do know that I don't think it's fair when people lose their hard-earned money. I don't want people to lose money. We've lost money in past business ventures – we almost went bankrupt once – and we've lost money in the markets, at a time when we couldn't afford to lose any.

Steve and I were buying our first house on Sunshine Coast and the stock market started tanking, so we pulled money out of our retirement savings plan as fast as we could because we were literally losing money every day! That's when we first started questioning the traditional method of savings and questioning our knowledge on how money works. It's amazing how fast you pick up financial knowledge when your money is disappearing!

We help people now because we learned from going through life's challenges. We want to help others to avoid that. Everybody goes through adversity. In life, there are moments of utter joy and moments of deepest despair. To know happiness is to know sadness or there would only be one state of being. You will go through adversity, so you need to know how to not only survive it but thrive despite it.

There's enough adversity in life; money shouldn't be one of them. Challenges happen. Loved ones will pass away, they will get sick, there will be losses and failures in life but if I can help one aspect of that through what I know, I will. This is true even in our business where we help people set up their financial lives. I want to help others get through those tough times a little easier, and that's why I do what I do.

What inspired me to make the decision to do what I do

I can't pinpoint one thing that inspired me to make the choices I did, to decide to do what I do. It was an entire life that led up to it. And, it would take an entire book to go into it all, maybe even in a few volumes! So, I'll whittle it down to an event, a few key people, and a book.

We had a very successful business venture, worth a few million dollars, and things looked pretty rosy. Steve and I built it quickly, but about 3 years into it, we saw our business market starting to change. We could see what we were doing might be phased out because of new and upcoming technological trends. We browsed through business ideas online and in franchise magazines. We found one that looked promising and fun to take on. We researched it heavily, went to all the professionals, and everybody said it looked good on paper – but unfortunately reality can present a very different scenario.

We both soon realized what we thought was a good investment of our time, energy and money, turned out to be a very bad decision— particularly financially. Just a year into it, Steve and I were losing so much money, we decided we had to get out as quickly as possible before we lost everything we had worked so hard to get. We had to start liquidating our assets and our house might have to be included because we couldn't see how we could continue to afford to live there.

Fortunately, we pulled all our resources together with the guidance of a dear friend who also recommended a financial software solution that used the principle of cash flow to pay off our debt. That same friend sent us a book. A book that would impact our lives so much, it changed our career paths. It was Pamela Yellen's book, Bank on Yourself.

That's when we discovered how to use participating whole life to protect one's whole family in case something happens, like a death. But we also discovered the living benefits aspect to it, the equity that builds up into what is called the cash surrendered value. That cash value builds up over time as you pay your policy and can be used to fund life's purchases or pay off debt.

Going through times of adversity

I've been through a lot of adversity. For me, being faced with bankruptcy was pretty scary, but it wouldn't be the be-all and end-all. It certainly isn't the worst thing I've been through! I've been very poor and on welfare. I've had serious health conditions, even before my recent one with cancer. It all made me look at life differently. So when our family was faced with this financial disaster, Steve and I thought, "We've got this issue, we're faced with adversity, we're probably going to lose everything—how are we going to survive?" For me, I had intuitively thought that way, "How am I going to survive? I know I'll get through it. It might not be fun or pleasant, and it will likely be scary, but I'll get through it.

I started out in adversity. I was born with a heart condition that would not be identified until my 20s. While I was studying at university, my condition worsened enough that I needed surgery. I couldn't work during that time, let alone return to school. Fortunately, my surgery was a complete success.

Right before my time at university, I had been married to a man that didn't treat me very well. I found myself on my own with nowhere to live and a suitcase of possessions in the cab of my truck as I prepared for my first week of school and a new job I had just landed before fleeing my marriage. My life was literally turned upside down and in what seemed like the blink of an eye, my life was entirely different.

I grew up in a low-income family, so I learned about financial struggles from an early age. My family shopped at thrift stores well before it became trendy because we had to. I think it was for my 7th birthday, my mom gave me a beautiful royal blue bike with a banana seat and handle bars with tassels! I had never had a new one! I loved that bike! I can still see it in my mind, even though I owned it only for a week. We lived in an apartment building, and I had locked it up to grab some lunch before heading out again. Upon my return, I saw that someone had cut the lock cable and stolen my bike. My mom, a single parent at the time, could not afford to replace it but someone gave me a bike to use. I can tell you I remember that bike too, it was old and rusty, but at least I had something to ride.

I know the things that come up for people, and if you're taken care of financially, it's one less thing you have to worry about. There are enough struggles in life without having to worry about your finances. So when we were close to bankruptcy, that urgency "to know" kicked in again. It became very obvious that although I had more financial knowledge than the last time we were in trouble, it wasn't enough. I could manage the creditors, but I didn't know enough to make this situation work very well for me, so I set out to learn how to keep us away from bankruptcy.

How we overcame this problem

We had to learn very quickly to save as much money as we could. To pay down as many creditors as we could but in amounts that would keep them happy and allow more room to spread out what money we did have. One good thing was our credit score. It was still intact and still quite respectable. We had managed to make all our payments. But we were right on that cusp. If we didn't change something or do something, if we just sat there and waited, we would have gone under. It's like looking for a life preserver when you fear you may drown. We started talking to friends and realized we weren't the only ones going through tough times. The stock market was bad, and people were losing money, so we weren't the only business owners having a tough time.

We talked to a friend in the States, and he taught us how cash works in the world of finance. How banks use cash, how they invest their money, how to identify interest rates, how you can pay off things at opportune times so you're using it to the best leverage you can, and how to shift money around to leverage it better. Sometimes it seemed like we were taking from Paul to pay Peter, but it worked. It was all about knowing how things connect and how you can move money on certain days at certain amounts to make it all work to your benefit rather than that of the creditors.

We sought out a good accountant and lawyer to give us advice on cash flow and understanding what our options were. We protected ourselves in case something happened to us. We read Pamela Yellen's book and learned in a hurry how to use whole life insurance to pay off our debt. Then we built up our equity in our whole life policy so we could take that money out as a policy loan, a line of credit against the equity in our cash value to pay off our debt. We just kept chipping at it.

Fortunately, before venturing into our oh-so-doomed business, we had hired the help of a lawyer who had expertise in the business we were taking on. He told us to make sure we incorporated our company so that if we experienced a loss, we could write it off in the future and our personal assets would have more protection. Crucial advice that would save our bacon!

Now faced with a failed business and mounting bills, we had to find a way to make money. The very financial software we were using to get us out of debt was also our career a solution for the time being. We had learned so much about it that we decided to sell it and teach people what we knew. While we floated on our new venture, still chipping away at debt, we read more on Pamela Yellen's concept, Bank on Yourself, and others like it: Nelson Nash's *Becoming Your Own Banker* and Garrett Gunderson's *Killing Sacred Cows*, amongst others. The more we learned, the more passionate we became about helping others take control of their financial life. That was the start of the very successful businesses we have today. So from adversity came need and from need came opportunity and from opportunity came success.

My internal resources

As I mentioned, I love research, and I love learning. It's not something I thought I would have been drawn to as a child because of my dyslexia. Despite discouraging words from others, I did go to university. To prove them wrong, I stayed there for 9 years! Well, not really. I absolutely loved my studies, and of course, there were some adversities that kept me there longer. During that time, I had to discover how I learned because there was no one to turn to to show me. I had to figure out how I could stay in academia and thrive.

I have always tried to stay positive, not to say that I didn't have my moments. We had some scary days where the whole world felt like it was not just resting on our shoulders but bearing down on us, trying to push us to the ground and bury us. How I started my day was important. It's not like I woke up and said, "This is going to be the best day ever!" I woke up thinking, "It just is what it is and it's a good day". Sometimes it feels easier to be in a bad mood but I always found the days that I didn't approach with welcoming gratitude to be quite tough and dark.

When my son was born, I had made the decision to welcome him to his day with a big smile, a good morning exclamation and wrap him in my arms—even on days I didn't feel like it. You may feel like crap on the inside, but if you make yourself get up, smile at your family and hug them, it's amazing how quickly that feeling can disappear. It's mind over matter, and my whole life has always been that way. I didn't grow up with the resources many people had, we were poor but I had my mind, and it was rich. No amount of money gets your mind to that place. It may pay for a parking spot, but unless you're living with that mindset, you'll just be towed under.

For me, it was about perspective. I analyse things a lot. It sometimes seems constantly, for the good or the bad. If I can see things in my mind, then I can take the steps I need. I'm a big planner, and I see connections where many people don't. I contemplate different scenarios in my mind, assessing situations and anticipating my best decision depending on how I see a scenario actually pans out. In other words, I have a plan A, B, C and often a D and an E. Taking a high-level approach and pulling it apart to find the details so I can plan my next moves—it's rather like playing chess and trying to plan for several moves beyond your opponent.

Information is power. I didn't wait for things to happen, I made them happen. But there were times I didn't. What I mean here is, as I was looking for a solution or trying to make something happen, I would run into so many stumbling blocks, it would make me stop to consider if I was doing the right thing. I would take a step back and think, perhaps this shouldn't happen, and you need to take another direction. All good plans are made to be broken. I found rigidity in life often led to unhappiness. Compromise was the order of most days. Mindfulness and self-awareness along with the attitude that I will get through this adversity and I will take from it what I can, learn what I can learn, is what won the day.

Steve had already been through a lot of personal development, having learned about thinking processes and self-help. We made a good team. We also had support in what we were doing from friends. I don't think our family really knew what was going on. Admittedly, some people thought we were crazy. It's still astonishing to me to look back and think how neither of us worked much for almost a year. We were busy learning! We were working enough to make our payments on our bills, and just doing what we had to do. We had plans, but if opportunities came along that seemed to be a good fit, we made an adjustment, and we had open minds. If it earned us money, we did it. If we had to sell it, we sold it. We just did what we had to, to get through.

Sometimes people come across adversity, but they aren't doing what they need to do in order to keep things afloat. Often a sacrifice is needed. As tough as it is, it's the way to freedom. We did think of selling our house and were willing to do that if all else failed. We created a plan, that if things didn't turn around by a certain date, then the house would go up for sale. We did end up keeping our house, but we sold things like our travel trailer and a piece of recreational land we had purchased some years back. Just those two things brought in about $40,000. Garage sales and clothing consignment stores brought in some more money.

Another time when my car broke down and we couldn't afford the $2000 repair, we sold it as-is for the most money we could get for it; we bought a car for a few hundred dollars and used the leftover money to pay another bill. That car is etched in my lungs. It was so dusty I could barely breathe. I had to drive with my windows open and all the interior lights were burned out, so we couldn't drive at night. The floor boards had rusted out, and the road was visible through them. It was akin to a glass bottom boat but not nearly as endearing or interesting! It's a simple example, but we had to make sacrifices in life to get through things. If it meant that things had to be sold or a tough decision had to be made, then that's what happened. Tough now doesn't mean tough forever. Steve and I knew that we could make money; we did it. We built up a whole bunch of equity, we made a whole bunch of money, and then we lost it. That's life. Life is full of ups and downs.

Not long ago during a conversation with a friend, she said, "I just want to live happily ever after," and I said, "There is no happily ever after. That's a falsehood. We go through ups and downs." That's what life is, and it's how you get through those ups and downs that make you content in life. There are sad moments, and there are happy moments. You can't live in the extreme happiness all the time. You don't go anywhere if you do that. If you're so busy being happy, you can't do anything else. If you're so busy being sad, you can't do anything else. There are things that will bring you down for a long time. I'm not saying people need to pull themselves out immediately.

It's about working through it for however long it takes. Recognizing what is going on and working through it. It may not be easy, just doable.

Time is also a consideration. I often think people expect a tough time should be solved and disappear overnight. It can take years to work through an adversity, particularly if there are several others peppered in along the way. Losing that business and putting everything on the line to change our lives, took years to do. We didn't become successful in the blink of an eye. All this happened a decade ago.

There are other losses in life that are even tougher to manage. Money is money, you lose it and you make it, you lose and you make it again. Dealing with a critical illness or the loss of a child, those are adversities that are much tougher to deal with. I've witnessed incredible strength to carry on in those circumstances. I had my own illness to deal with. Would the cancer I had take my life or would the complications from the treatment take me first? What should have taken several months to go through actually took a few years. I can't even pin the word recover to it. I didn't go back to the person I was. I think the most impactful realization I have had is, it's not about recovering so much as it is able accept a changed life and the person one becomes after going through adverse times.

The most important lesson I learned

Perseverance or stick-to-it-iveness in relation to mindset is the most important lesson I learned. In my darkest hours, people would often say to me, "You're so strong". I find it tough to think of myself in those terms. Instead what is going through my mind is, "I just did what I had to do." I had to persevere; the option not to wasn't conceivable to me.

To be honest, when I was going through cancer, I would have a pity party every once in a while. I stayed in the Pity Hotel for a night or two and then I checked out. I didn't live there. I let myself go through the self-pity, experience it and learn from it. The days I was full of pity were not much fun. I had some pretty horrible days and some beyond my control due to medications and whatnot. But when I could control it, I did. It was easier to smile and take on my day with gratitude than to be filled with despair and fear.

Adversity has fear in it. Fear of what is going on and how you will work through it. Fear of how your life will look when it is done. Adversity bothers us so much because we're afraid of what's going on. Think: "How can I change my situation and how can I get through this? If I stay here, it's not going to change, and I'm going to be afraid forever. Or, I can make the choice in how to get out of this." You have the power to persevere.

Recommended books:

"The Bank on Yourself Revolution", Pamela Yellen

"Becoming Your Own Banker", Nelson Nash

"Killing Sacred Cows", Garrett Gunderson

"What would the Rockefellers Do?", Michael Isom and Garrett Gunderson

"Simple Success Strategies for Women Entrepreneurs", Michele Devlin et al.

"Transform Your Life, Business & Health". Brian Tracey and Stephen Devlin, et al.

"The Secret to Lifetime Financial Security", Stephen Devlin and Pamela Yellen, et al.

The religious or spiritual book of your choice.

About the Author, Michele Devlin

CEO and Chief Compliance Officer of
MacDev Financial Group Corp
Email: michele@macdevfinancial.com
Phone: 604-512-4889
www.macdevfinancial.com
www.findoutmorenow.ca
www.bankonyourself.com
www.infinitebanking.org
www.wealthfactory.com

Michele Platje Devlin is the Chief Executive Officer (CEO) and Chief Compliance Officer of MacDev Financial Group Corp. co-founded with her husband, Stephen Devlin. More recently they established SET Financial Solutions Inc., home of the Bank on Yourself™ concept for Canada. Michele and Stephen are highly regarded in their industry and hold several awards, along with their dedicated team of advisors across the country. Michele's ultimate vision is to empower women to take control of their finances with safe and effective strategies that serve and protect them in life, wealth and legacy. Financial Control for Life!

Michele is a consummate entrepreneur and has held various executive titles over her professional career, which was built on her education and expertise in continuity planning, business and government operations, public and corporate policy as well as compliance and privacy regulations. Under Michele's leadership during her three-year term as President of the Gibsons and District Chamber of Commerce and directorship from 2009-2013, the Chamber built a Visitor's Information Park to greet travelers upon their arrival on the Sunshine Coast. This collaborative community project developed from a sustainable financial framework created by Michele and her team. In 1999, Michele and three partners formed Concept Plus Risk Management Group, an analytical policy planning consulting company specializing in risk management. As Director of Risk Management, she strategically managed policy initiatives and project management cases that included response to 9-11 and anthrax threats.

Early in her career, she held a prestigious research associate position with the Department of Economics at Simon Fraser University from 1997-2001. In this role, she provided research, editing and writing support to faculty members on various academic publications in multiple disciplines. By 2006, her contribution to the book Economic Transformations: General Purpose Technologies and Long Term Economic Growth with Dr. Richard Lipsey was published. Michele holds a degree from Simon Fraser University in Communication and Geography, with a special interest in Economics. A scholarship award sent her to study abroad—earning her international certificates in Strategic Management of Technology in a Global Environment from the Politecnico di Milano and in Strategic Management of Telecommunications in a Global Environment from the Helsinki University of Technology.

Today Michele splits her time between homes in Vancouver and the Sunshine Coast of British Columbia with her husband and business partner Stephen Devlin and their teenage son. As a colorectal cancer veteran, her passion project is managing the Facebook page *Literally Kicking Cancer in the Ass,* aimed at raising awareness and informing the public about the disease. In her downtime, she enjoys spending time with her family, traveling, kayaking, skiing and walking along the beach. She has a natural curiosity about life, the environment and the experiences that shape modern society and is an active life-long learner. Her family is her greatest pride and joy.

The Art of BALANCE

By Rhona Parsons

When I was a teenager, I was very active in my life; a track and field participant in school, a netball player, and I always loved to dance. After being made to move to Canada with my family when I was 15, I became very depressed and resentful to my parents for uprooting me from my home country and I stopped being active, not participating in any form of exercise. After giving birth to my first beautiful baby girl at the age of 19, I began walking a little and after my marriage split up, I was left without a vehicle so walking became my primary mode of transportation.

When I met my (now) husband Brian, he was an avid gym goer. I joined the gym he went to and he taught me how to lift weights. After a couple of months, my friend Hester and I began meeting 3x a week for a workout; I loved the changes I was feeling in my body! I was getting stronger and feeling great but also knew I had to do a cardio component to keep my heart healthy and to get my body fitter. I hated the thought of being on a treadmill for an hour at a time (I never did enjoy running in school), so I joined an Aerobics class. As I began to learn the moves and see more changes in my body, I thought, "Wow, this beats the treadmill any day! It's just like dancing! I could become an aerobics instructor and get paid for doing cardio!" and so I began the journey that would feed my passion to help others.

I lived in Prince Rupert, a north-western town in BC, and I couldn't get to Vancouver to attend any teacher trainings so I learned to teach by watching videos of Karen Voight, a fitness expert from the USA. I studied and practiced so much, that on the day of my practical exam, 1 nailed it, teaching 9 instructors who had signed up for my class! I loved my new career and wanted to learn more about the body so I soon became a Personal Trainer. I loved helping others with their fitness and health goals, and in 1999, I decided I wanted to pursue a career in Physiotherapy so I went back to school and completed my Grade 11 and 12 Sciences and Math. It was during my first semester at College that I realized this was a one chance deal and it wasn't going to happen; I was 38 and would be applying for University at age 40. I needed an A+ average, there were only 35 seats available at University, and I also had 2 teens at home that needed me more than they thought I did. It was a hard decision to make, but no sooner than I made it, Stott Pilates began showing up in every media that I looked at; I realized this was the way I could help others! The course was in Vancouver but was $800; money that I didn't have. I did have me though, and for the last 3 years I had been teaching Yoga. I asked around and found a room that was offered to me for free. I created a 6-week yoga session and made $717! I had my money for the course!

My husband was very supportive of my decision, and once I found a place to rent, he helped me renovate and bring my studio to fruition. In September 2000 I opened my first Pilates/Yoga Studio; BODYWORKS Fitness & Health Studio. I could finally do what I wanted to do; help others get the best out of life through self-care.

The Chapters of Adversity

I was born in a very small village, Kingsclere, that is situated in Hampshire in the south of England; I have 2 older brothers and a younger sister. We were surrounded by many relatives, but unfortunately, our families were divided by favourite grandchildren and children. I wasn't one of the favourite grandchildren or child, and so I don't remember many happy times as a child, just a lot of wishing that I was the favourite so I could shine brightly and be surrounded by the love that I craved.

Do you know that our thoughts come from only one of two places: fear or love? Under the title of fear are the feelings of sadness, anger, frustration, loneliness, disappointment, etc., and when I look back at my life, I realize that I have been living in fear since I was 9 years old; ever since my best friend left the village that we lived in. Anne's father was the local vicar so I attended church and Sunday school with her. I was very lost and lonely when Anne left and really didn't have any other friends. I continued going to church though, and when I began attending Secondary School at age 11, I became friends with a group of girls from the village. Unfortunately for most of us, we were all bullied by the leader of our group through the 4 years of school; if she didn't like you, no one was allowed to. I was so unhappy that I ran away when I was 12 but that didn't really change anything. I put up with being bullied until I was 15 and then life became even more hellish; my parents took me and two of my siblings and immigrated to Canada. Who moves their 15-year old daughter to another country and to a small town that was on the other side of Canada? Thank God for my English accent! I was constantly surrounded by people wanting to hear me talk, and I was grateful for the friends I made, but my heart was so broken from being disconnected from my family and the new friends I had finally made before I left, that I spent a lot of time alone.

I met my first husband at secondary school and fast forward a marriage, a baby, a separation, 2 more children and finally a divorce. I was once again alone, but this time with my 3 beautiful girls. My parents helped out immensely and my eldest daughter was my angel; she helped me so much looking after her sisters (Ky, I am forever grateful). I finally had some amazing friends in my life that were there for me and my girls. Even though I was surrounded by love and support of my family, friends and children, I was living in a constant state of fear, trying always to get ahead. Don't get me wrong, my daughters gave me many happy, cherished moments, and I did the best that I could for them; looking back, though, I struggled being a single mom and spiraled downwards into a depression. Lucky for me, once again, I had a fantastic doctor who helped me by listening and gave me great advice; my wonderful friends picked me up, brought me back to the present with their loving matter-of-fact lectures and today, I know I did the best that I could with the tools that I had and am truly grateful for those wonderful people who supported, loved and helped me.

I met Brian through this time in my life, and eventually we married in 1993. Life continued, and we moved to Vernon in 2003 after the local pulp mill had closed down and Brian was in search for work after going back to school for a year. Our children had grown and left home, so it was just him and I; the first time that we were alone together since our first date in 1987. I was teaching full time, and Brian was hired by the city to work with the city Fire Department. Life was great…until March 2006 when Brian came home from the gym one day and told me that he wasn't feeling very well. He went for a nap and fast forward almost 2 years later, after his health had deteriorated so much that he wasn't able to work, he had a heart transplant at St. Paul's Hospital in Vancouver. During those 2 years, I was working at a local fitness centre in a management position. I had 15 instructors working for/with me, and I was personal training plus working full time at home (Brian was unable to do any chores around the house). I was taking another 500-hour yoga course and had my Yoga, Pilates and meditation classes that were keeping me from crashing. To top it off, our beautiful 14-year old cat went missing on one of the prior trips to the hospital. There was so much sadness in our home. Looking back, I was living fully in the present moment; I was running full speed ahead and my cortisol levels were going at full steam!

Immediately following Brian's successful surgery, I fell ill for 10 days and finally surrendered, coming home and taking time for me. During Brian's recovery, we had huge support from both our workplaces and even though I was surrounded by love and support from my colleagues and clients, I left my career in 2010 due to an injury that stopped me from teaching any of my classes. I believe that our emotions do affect our health and my health was in trouble (even though I didn't know it at the time), and it showed up as Achilles Tendonitis in both ankles. During rehab (obviously not listening to my body) and without the support of my husband, I marched forward and opened a fitness studio with 2 partners.

Unknowingly, our marriage was in trouble as Brian and I were completely disconnected. With the stress of my failing marriage and a stressful business from being new and that had opened late due to construction, I was spiraling downward emotionally very fast without realizing it. I was stressed to the max. I felt so sad every day and I dreaded coming home. One evening in August 2012, after having cried for most of the day, I sat in my hot tub, looked up at the sky and said to the Universe "I'm ready...bring it on". I was exhausted and just wanted my life to change. I had no idea what was going to happen, but something had to. A week later, I left my husband and a month later, my business; I headed into an emotional/nervous breakdown. I was in a state of Adrenal Exhaustion; I was done. I couldn't help anyone with their journeys, let alone help me...and so...I...surrendered.

Even though I was in this very dark place, I wasn't afraid because I knew I was being looked after and guided. It was where I needed to be; the Phoenix had died and was waiting to be reborn.

Moving into the Positive

For the next few months, after getting back on my feet, I had to make some very important decisions because I knew that I needed to de-stress my life if I wanted happiness and fulfillment.

The most important decision I had to make was about my relationship with my husband. Brian and I realized we wanted to work on our relationship – a new relationship as the other one we knew was gone...finished. We still loved each other very much, so we began to rebuild our relationship very slowly. It has now been 4 years since we moved back in with each other. No, it hasn't been easy. When you have been with someone for a long time, almost 30 years for us, it's very easy to get back into the old groove. When this happens, I bring it to Brian's attention, and together, we change our course of action. Our love is strong, and our commitment to each other is a lifetime one.

I began to meditate more and began reading many self-help books that have helped me understand who, as a human being, I really am and what I'm made of. It took me 2 ½ years with the help of very special friends and a local female doctor who specializes in female hormones for me to feel 'normal' again; happy and alive!

"Be the change you want to see in the world"

- Gandhi

I've learned, and believe, that I am a spiritual being having a human existence and we are here on this earth to serve others, but more importantly, to live our lives to the fullest through love and happiness; that the families we are in and the people we meet are here for reasons beyond our comprehension. People do come into our lives for a reason, a season or a lifetime, either to learn from us or for us to learn from them. I also believe that we get to choose many things and these choices will bring us what we ask for and believe in!

You keep believing that you are poor and have no money? You will always be poor and broke.

You believe that you are stuck in the crappy job? You will always have the same job.

You want to continue to stay and live in an unhappy relationship? You will.

You see, we do get to choose our life and circumstances (I am not talking physical illnesses here – that's another chapter) but to live our life to the fullest, we need to choose what we want and then take radical action to make it happen. We need to begin thinking positive thoughts, surrounding ourselves with positive people, and taking positive action!

Have you heard the saying "Misery loves company"? It's so true and when you begin to surround yourself with positive people, those negative, pessimistic people will gradually disappear out of your life. Did they bring something to your life? Absolutely…so thank them for what they brought, wish them well and let them go.

Today I am in a much happier place and looking forward to great things! I live each day with happiness in my heart and strive to live with happy thoughts. Do I get sad, angry and/or frustrated? You bet I do. The difference is, when I begin to feel something other than happiness, I have a little chat with myself. I ask the questions: "What is truly going on here? Why am I feeling this way? What can I do to let it pass?" Sometimes I have to surrender into the feelings - feel the anger, the hurt or sadness so that I can move through it back to feeling happy and fulfilled once again. All those hurts that I felt and the belief systems that were formed in me from the tender age of 4 and up are still part of me and still come to the surface once in a while. When they do I can now recognize them and let them go. We are able to change our mindsets and belief systems, and when some old feeling arises and I'm not able to figure it out by myself, I have a coach and mentor who I call upon to help me through it. Some of these feelings are embedded so deep in our unconscious minds that we need outside help to shift them.

At the end of each and every class I teach, I leave my participants with the following quote:

"Have a great day unless you choose otherwise"

138

You see, it is your choice! Are you going to have a great day? Only you can decide whether you will or not. I wish you one from the bottom of my heart.

"When the power of love overcomes the love of power, the world will attain peace"

- Jimi Hendrix

About the Author, Rhona Parsons

Bodyworks Fitness & Health
Vernon, BC
Website: www.bodyworksbms.com
Email: pilates4life@hotmail.com
Phone: 250-308-8616
Facebook: https://www.facebook.com/vernonbodyworksbms

As an entrepreneur, Life Coach, a student of the Mind, Body & Spirit theory, and a National Fitness Presenter and Yoga Instructor, Rhona "lights up" guiding and instructing others to live their best life. She has followed her love and passion for helping others by developing and teaching fitness and yoga programs for over 20 years. Rhona is a highly accomplished National Bender Ball Master Trainer and loves teaching a variety of classes; she has mentored many instructors by developing and teaching Continuing Education approved workshops.

Rhona also teaches Pilates and Pfilates (Pelvic Floor Pilates), and is a Personal and Group Fitness Trainer specializing in Core and Posture helping people with balance and stability and as a Life Coach, helping people to bring balance into their lives.

Rhona is a caring, passionate person who loves her work. She is a unique and focused individual and constantly upgrades her skills to be able to teach and help others. Incredible focus and dedication to her beliefs are always evident and her ability to motivate clients through her vast knowledge is truly inspiring. Boundless energy, terrific time management talents and a great sense of humour all add to her capabilities. Rhona is a highly motivated, fun, kind, knowledgeable, physically fit, caring, loving individual. She is a clear, concise and methodical instructor who motivates others to take care of themselves and be kind to each other. Rhona lives her truth by balancing her dedication to her career and clients, and her devotion to her family and their wellbeing as well as to the wellbeing of everyone who asks for help.

Rhona offers a free 60-minute consultation to everyone who is looking for a new change in his/her life through fitness, health and/or wellness.

From Self-Saboteur to Self-Empowered Entrepreneur

By Rosa Livingstone

"And the day came when the risk to remain tight in a bud was more painful than the risk it took to blossom." This quote by Anais Nin is one that has spoken to me and impacted me profoundly over the years. There are many moments when pain overrode my fear of blossoming, and a major one was in 2008 when I grabbed my backbone, pushed back my fear of failing and started believing in myself.

I came into this world to immigrant Portuguese parents in 1964. My Dad was a fisherman and my mother a homemaker until I was six years old. I had a wonderful elder sister.

I've had next to no recall of the first eight years of my life until recovering memories with Hypnotherapy 11 years ago so what I knew about myself was based on comments passed down by my Mom. I don't have baby pictures because they couldn't afford a camera, so as a child, I thought I was adopted and my sister reinforced it when she wanted to tease me.

Mom seemed to regale in telling stories about how I was the ugliest baby born, all skin and bone, with a full head of straight black hair and long, paddle-like feet. She knew I'd never drown! She said that when I was born, my Dad had expected to have a son and everyone thought she looked like she was 'carrying' a boy so he was convinced and happy in his expectation. But he was so angry when he heard he'd had another daughter that he didn't see my Mom nor meet me until a day after I was born, standing at the door to her hospital room, silently glaring, as if it was her fault the beloved boy was a skinny-assed girl. I guess he didn't know that men determine a child's gender. Thus began my perception of being unlovable, rejected and abandoned.

We moved to a small northern B.C. town in a tiny two-bedroom home with a suite below where my maternal grandparents lived. I don't recall much discord or violence between my parents in my early childhood. But there was. Portuguese men take their role seriously – keep the wife and kids in line. Dad had a volatile and explosive temper and what gave us a breather from his constant wrath was that he was away fishing a lot. Yeah, salmon and herring!

My Mom always seemed tired and depressed, beginning with her coming to this country to find it a challenging place. She couldn't speak the language to ask for what she needed in the grocery store and was often too embarrassed to shop because she had to point to the items she needed and she'd mispronounce words. A bag of chips became a bag of "shits" which caused the shop owner, Doug (whom she called "Dog") to snicker. This life was a disappointment to her because in Portugal, she was born in a lovely town on the seaside with warm weather to ease her days under the rule of typically strict parents. She barely knew my Dad when they married. Although not an arranged marriage, my grandparents opposed it because his family was poor. But she married him because the other girls swooned over him – a handsome, green eyed, strawberry blond. Once she married, she saw a different person; he was an angry and insecure man. She also inherited her widowed Father-in-Law to care for. This was a lot for a young bride.

I can only recall my Mom ever playing with me once, drawing stick people on a stark piece of white paper. To me, this gesture meant the world. She loved me! But it didn't happen again. She was always busy working, cooking or cleaning. My idol was my sister, who made dresses for my Barbie dolls, peanut butter muffins and looked after me when my Mother went to work.

But I also grew up in her shadow. Mom always compared me to her – how she was obedient, calm, and she listened. And when my sister left home at 18, I was compared to every other European daughter. Yes, I was a fierce bundle of energy that she had no idea what to do with. I recall the freedom of summer, running with glee in the woods with my friends and hearing her or my sister calling me in for dinner. And I'd ignore them, squeezing the last bit of fun out of dusk. I'd get punished afterwards but it was worth it. This was my taste of independence; playing in the streets, running full speed up and down hills until finally getting my first bicycle at age nine thanks to my wonderful Grandfather. I had more scabs on my legs than any other kid I knew, and I wore them with pride. It drove my Mom crazy! Why couldn't I play at home quietly and not hang upside down from trees?

Mom was jealous of the close relationship I had with my sister (and still do). I did love her more because she paid attention to me and was my 'real" Mom. Mom learned to play us against each other in order to control us. What I see now, as a grown woman, is that she was depressed, repressed, angry, and frustrated and craved the validation and love she never felt in her childhood. And my Dad certainly didn't help with any of that.

At nine, my beloved Grandparents returned to Portugal, and I tasted abandonment like a sour lemon. Grandpa was the man in my life, who showed me love by playing and cuddling with me. Then my carefree time ended when I was ten when my sister secretly shared with me that she wasn't returning from a vacation in Portugal; she was escaping the imprisonment of my Dad's rule. I felt the deepest sadness in my heart.

My parents were under the assumption my sister was returning after the summer vacation. But she wrote in August, 1974, that she wasn't and instead, getting married and wanted their blessing. My Mom saw and read the letter first and left it for Dad, taking me out shopping. I recall how skittish she was that afternoon and my feeling an unknown dread creeping into my chest. When we arrived home, Dad was furiously waiting. I can't describe what happened as it's still too terrifying to recall but I stood watching, frozen in place, helpless and paralyzed, as this horror scene unfolded that no child should witness, all because he felt Mom had conspired with my sister about this marriage, which Mom had not. His own powerlessness at not being able to control my sister made him nuts! Mom took the punishment without a sound nor a whimper. I don't recall when her ordeal stopped or where Dad went afterwards but I took her into my bedroom and comforted her. Then and there began my hatred and fear of my father for there was more to come over the years. I learned quickly how dysfunctional our family truly was. No one knew about the spousal violence. It was under the "Code of Secrecy."

With my sister as a shield gone, I assumed all her responsibilities, and I grew up fast. My days of freedom disappeared like the setting sun on my childhood. I now had to help Mom clean the house, translate government forms, and take her to doctor appointments. There was no choice, and I found myself in a prison. My life became school and home as both parents were strict. My ethic of hard work today began then. At 10, I started babysitting summers to save money for the things I wanted, which my Mom wouldn't buy because she thought they were frivolous. I had the necessities. I'd learned their belief that you must work hard, keep your job until retirement for the pension, pay cash to buy what you need, eat out only on a very special occasion, and save your money for your old age! At 12, I faked my ID to work in a fishing cannery with my Mom to make the 'big bucks". I gave up summers to spend 10 - 12 hours standing at a trough cleaning out gutted salmon. And I learned to save like nobody's business. I tasted a bit of freedom again having my own bank account. Hello, first pair of leather pants at 14!

I can look back now and pinpoint many events that shaped who I am. I can recall very little positive attention from my parents, next to nothing in physical demonstrations of love towards me, only criticism, comparison, and anger. I was always fearful of doing or saying the wrong thing. Mom taught me that girls were meant to get married once and to someone who would support her, give her a position in life, have his children and run a home like a boot-camp. Appearances were everything. And if he mistreated you, oh well. It's the wife's job to suck it up.

So I rebelled from an instinctual place that remembered how it felt to be free. I just wanted to be loved and accepted for me! Somewhere along the way, I believed that if I were perfect (which is what my Mom wanted me to be), then I'd be loved. It showed up in my scholastic achievements, getting straight A's., excelling and rewarded for my brain. I had to be the best in sports, until my parents no longer allowed me to participate in high school because team travelling to other cities meant I might leave behind my virginity. I wore a mask throughout my career life until my early 40's, terrified of being shamed; shamed at not being good enough, capable enough, intelligent enough, pretty enough nor worthy enough.

Because I grew up with drama, it was part of my makeup and I subconsciously created it in my relationships with men. I married at 19, not to escape my parents but to feel loved. And I subconsciously chose someone who was jealous and insecure like my Dad. I left after two years.

I married again at 26 and thought that this time I'd gotten it right. Wrong! He was another controller who loved the idea of me but not necessarily who I was. I left after seven years and became a single mother to a four-year-old son.

My next relationship lasted 11 years. We fought constantly, never seeing eye-to-eye. My relationships were a study in what not to do versus what was healthy. I began to realize that my belief that I could change someone was utterly false and that maybe I was choosing men who reminded me of my Dad. What an eye opener! I left again with my eldest and a seven-year-old son.

It wasn't until I began to train as a Clinical Hypnotherapist in 2006 that I began to explore my beliefs, my perceptions, my habits and my choices. It was a defining moment, leading me to start healing myself and understanding my gifts and the unique traits I could bring to the world. It was hard work stripping myself down naked and having to face all the things that I'd done to reinforce shame and hurt myself. But it also sparked the passion I still feel strongly to help other women regain their power and occupy their rightful place in this world through my work and public speaking. I teach many workshops on empowerment and stopping self-sabotage. I even recently wrote my first book on the subject of how and why self-sabotage keeps us in a prison of our own making. I had to work through my own self-sabotage to write it.

Learning about what I subconsciously believed as true about my worth due to all my childhood experiences was when I began to challenge the toxic blueprint of expectations I carried around with me like a shadow everywhere I went. I started reclaiming that little Rosa inside who was so amazing yet so lost inside the darkness of her environment. I became determined to help her find her light, her spark, and to shine. I was also able to begin facing and overcoming the depression I'd lived with since being diagnosed at 21. I'd been medicated for 20 years, something I hid from only those I trusted.

Speaking of trust, this was the #1 issue that clouded my self-esteem and had me self-sabotaging all areas of my life. I didn't truly trust anyone with my heart. How could I if my parents let me down, rejected me through their words and actions, these two adults that I looked to in order to feel safe, validated and loved? If I wasn't enough to them, who would I be enough for? But guess what? It wasn't others I didn't trust. It was me I didn't trust! I forgot what it felt like to believe in myself as I once did as a little girl who was fearless, curious and headstrong. I rekindled that strength in 2008 when I had the courage to go out on my own with two boys, barely having started my own business, a few bucks in the bank and a belief that I could make a life for us knowing my safety net was me!

As soon as I believed in myself, the veil began to lift on what I could accomplish. I found reserves of determination I didn't know I had. I held it all together as my youngest son went through two 17- month rounds of Chemotherapy over a four year period to shrink a benign brain tumour discovered when he was four years old. I found the strength to believe I could make my Hypnotherapy business not only sustain itself but thrive, even when the closest to me didn't understand what the hell I was doing and questioned not staying in the safe career I'd had in the hotel industry, with benefits, for over 20 years. I doubled my income in my second year as an entrepreneur, never looking back and worked damn hard to do it. I learned I could!

I had the faith to believe I deserved a partner who would be my equal, who would accept me 'as is', completely 'flawsome', and stand beside me during the ups and downs of life. And I did. He's amazing.

I didn't come to this place of self-compassion, love and acceptance because I have special Wonder Woman gifts. I arrived here because within me was always that light of worthiness and I fought, faced and conquered many of my demons. Am I done? Hell no. Will I continue to go where it hurts to heal? Hell yes! Re-discovering your magnificence before the world told you otherwise is messy, emotional, painful, mascara-down-the-face crying work. And it's all worth it!

I'd like to share three thoughts about what I believe about life and that I wish for you:

Thought #1:

Imagine that life stretches ahead like a road. You can see that there are long and short roads; paved and unpaved roads; zigging and zagging roads. We all stand on many roads on this journey of life. There are roads that lead to fulfilling experiences but also roads that lead to sadness and loneliness, to sabotage and disappointment. Well, wonderful women, maybe you're standing on one now.

You can't know where a road will lead you until you take it! And whatever road you choose is the right one in that moment. There's always something to learn from where you came. And one of the most important things you need to realize about life is that there aren't any guarantees. Choosing to do the right thing all the time won't lead you to happiness. Loving someone with all your heart won't guarantee that it'll land you in a bed of roses or that it'll be reciprocated. Becoming successful and having loads of money won't guarantee happiness. There are too many possible outcomes, which you really can't control. The only thing you can control is the decisions that you'll make, after uncovering why they're important to you.

At your crossroads, you can go left, right, ahead or backwards. Which road will you take? Do any of them give you a guarantee that you'd choose the right one? Would you take any road, or just stand with feet planted at a crossroad?

Thought #2

We all rationalize our hurts. We blame others. We criticize ourselves for what we think we lack to make love and friendships 'stick'.

I believe fitting in and belonging are two different things. When we do cartwheels to please others to fit in, we are denying ourselves. We are like chameleons changing colour to fit in, and so not truly being ourselves. We deny our uniqueness. We show the face that we think others will like, be attracted to and accept.

Belonging is being YOU. It's showing up in the world as your authentic and best self regardless of what others think. It's embracing all the things that make you 'you". To be authentic, you have to know yourself. And to know yourself, you have to dig deep and face all those thoughts, actions and behaviours that you dislike about yourself. I think it's a labour of love and you're worth it!

149

Thought #3

I believe that the most damaging side effect of being abused, betrayed, ridiculed or abandoned is how we come to see ourselves through the eyes of our pain. It damages our self-esteem because we are seeing ourselves as our seeping wounds and not separate from them. We let what hurt us define us. It's like when we say, "I'm depressed" as a way of explaining how we feel. But we are not "depressed" as a whole person. It is a state of mind, one state of mind, yet we use it to blanket how we see ourselves. Someone who is depressed is also a mother, a father, a professional, a friend.

You might see yourself as "not enough" or a failure. When you start believing that if you were perfect and behaved perfectly, you'd finally be accepted, admired, and loved, things will only go to shit. The truth is, you're not perfect nor are you unworthy!! You are a whole, skilled, capable, loving, lovable and remarkable person. You always were and always will be. Isn't it time you believed it?

I find it mind blowing that who we think we are and the way we act and react to the world is a result of our early experiences. The way we look at ourselves, the way we look at the world and at life in general, is all based on what we learned in childhood. And all the hurts never went away. They are stored in the secret recesses of our inner mind, and they are reflected not only in how we feel and think about ourselves, but in what we expect from others. The shift happens when you begin to challenge your negative inner critic and the dribble it tells you, which will lead to changing your mindset, perspective and outlook about your place in the world. You have the ability to make the shift, to embrace the beautiful and 'perfectly imperfect' woman you are....so own it like a pair of Jimmy Choo kick-ass shoes and strut the catwalk of life!

Sending each of you a bright light, to illuminate the marvelous and spectacular woman you are. Make no excuses, stop procrastinating and be you! I'm committed to my light, and this attitude is full of rich opportunities. I pass the torch to you so it can bring light to your darkness so you, too, can shine.

About the Author, Rosa Livingstone

Website: www.aloadoffyourmind.com
www.selfsabotagingself.com
Phone: 778-238-2427
Email: aloadoffyourmind@telus.net
Facebook:: @MindCoaching101
 and @selfsabotagingself
Twitter: @MindCoaching101
Linkedin: https://ca.linkedin.com/in/rosa-livingstone-34b1b147

Rosa Livingstone is a Certified Clinical Hypnotherapist, Mind/Life Coach and Motivational Speaker/Teacher, the published author of "Self Sabotage: The Art of Screwing Up", as well a certified Hypnotherapy Instructor, located in Coquitlam, BC, Canada.

Rosa had spent over 20 years in the Management side of the Hospitality Industry, the last seven as a Director of Sales for a major Canadian Hotel chain. She had to suddenly reinvent herself after a medical incident with her Son, which left her unable to work in her demanding field. She had one driving thought in mind when faced with creating a new career direction – she had to help others, which has always been paramount in her philosophy on life.

Having discovered her passion in her career, she continues to believe she is called to coach, cajole, and encourage others to re-discover their inner un-tethered self. With over a decade of experience, she blends the science of the mind with the energy of the soul, using her spiritual perspective, along with her skills in trauma/belief system shifting, to help others that are willing and ready to discover their wings to fly!

Rosa believes that to have the life you have always deserved you have to face the emotional baggage that holds you back to create the space for self compassion, self worth and self trust. When she is not twisting herself in yoga poses, you'll find her writing, coaching, and cooking for her awesome husband and two fun-loving sons, while singing 80's tunes at the top of her lungs.

Never, Ever Give Up

By Jen Hickle

T he stage lights shone brightly. I crossed my legs and tucked them underneath me and sat up a little straighter on the couch provided for the panelists. There was nowhere I would rather be than on stage, speaking to hundreds of business owners. My passion radiated out of me, and I couldn't help making broad, dramatic motions with my hands, as I articulated the power of discipline and consistency as the catalyst for business growth. Scanning the crowd, I saw people furiously taking notes, some snapping pictures, and I realized how far I had come and all that I had accomplished.

After the conference session, I walked quickly out to the hotel lobby and stood behind my booth. Sales were going well, and a line of people stood waiting to schedule an appointment with me and my husband. I smiled. To be able to help so many business owners was a dream come true. And it wasn't too long ago that we were on government assistance and couldn't even afford to buy groceries. I snapped my attention back to the business owner in front of me. "How can I help you today?"

I've always loved being on stage. My parents were theatre directors and worship leaders and my mom was a school music teacher for most of my childhood. It was typical for me to sing a vocal solo or win a trophy for performing. A part of me comes alive when I'm on stage, whether I am speaking, singing, or playing the piano.

Halfway through my senior year of high school, I started teaching piano lessons to a few neighborhood kids. I fell in love with teaching immediately. When my mom approached me and said, "I have a way for you to pay for university-- you just have to teach 10 piano students every Saturday," it was a logical challenge. The only problem? I only had a handful of piano students. Where would I find more? This was my first introduction to marketing and advertising. Knowing very little, I hung up flyers at local schools, put a handmade yard sign in our front yard, stuffed mailboxes with more flyers, and started telling people I was accepting new students. It worked.

I filled up my Saturday schedule, started hiring other teachers to work for me, and although I missed out on weekend fun with my college friends, I graduated debt-free and walked the line, owning a little startup company. The new world of business suited me perfectly. I am not athletic at all, but I am competitive! If you give me a challenge, I'll rise to it. I'll put all my energy and effort into conquering it. If I am lacking knowledge, I'll research and figure it out. Step by step, I've found the answers I need to move forward to the next level. I've never given up.

My little handful of music students has slowly grown into a music school of 450 students and a staff of 25. Recently, my husband and I have expanded our company to help other music schools and various small businesses all over the United States, Canada and in the U.K. Using a proven system, we strategize ways to grow their business by improving their website, SEO, and online marketing.

Life is good. But it hasn't always been. And I've learned many lessons along the way.

1. Choose to rise above

At the young age of twenty, halfway through my music degree, I walked down the aisle to marry my high school sweetheart. I was finishing college and Chris was working as a youth pastor in a church. We knew finances would be tight, but we had no idea how hard things would really be. When our first baby came along just 3 years later, I knew growing my business was the key to getting out of low-income housing and into a real house of our own.

Every time Chris told me, "We can't afford that," I replied, "I'll get more students." And I did. I hired music teachers to work for me and I focused on the business administration, billing, scheduling, and marketing. We were living on a meager salary, but we were choosing to rise above our situation and create change. We didn't whine and complain. We didn't sit back, defeated, accepting of our situation. I got extremely creative at raising kids while growing a business, and I put all my effort into growing my little business.

While building my business in those early years, I was operating out of my natural comfort zone of talents and abilities, and this caused me a lot of frustration. I knew I had to keep pushing through, but life was hard. With four little kids, mountains of debt, no money (we were using government assistance for food each month), I lived for my nightly bath, just so I could slip under the scalding hot water and escape the world momentarily. One day, Chris told me that our water bill was too high and I needed stop taking so many baths. I looked at him incredulously. I was pregnant with baby #4 at the time and hot baths were the only pain relief for my sore body and stressed out mind. We had trimmed and cut the budget as much as possible and were living from paycheck to paycheck. I knew I had to make more money. Fast.

After my baby was born in January of 2008, the entire economy in the United States collapsed. My dad lost his job and I knew I had to do something to help. I took the risk of adding theatre classes to my music school and hired my parents to run it. Suddenly, everything was at stake. I knew I had to grow my company to help our financial situation, but I had no clue how. I was already working incredibly hard, reading every business book I could get my hands on, staying up late to enroll students, and frantically answering emails in any spare time that I could find.

Maybe success comes when you ignore your circumstances and just believe you can succeed, no matter what is stacked against you. In 2008, I chose to ignore the fact that everyone around me was losing their jobs and foreclosing on their homes. I chose to ignore that Rogers, a little suburb of Minneapolis, only has 10,000 people living in it. I looked on the bright side of things and focused on the 50,000 people surrounding Rogers who didn't have access to music lessons or theatre programs. Around that time, Time Magazine published an article stating that kids are the last expense parents cut out (they'll cut out eating out and buying luxury cars before changing their kids' lifestyle), so I decided that selling music lessons in a recession was a perfectly sane thing to do, even though everyone around me warned me that it was risky.

I started by making connections with other business owners in the area to find rehearsal space for our theatre classes. One connection led to another, and soon we had our own private studio space for music lessons in the back of a brand-new ballet school. The theatre classes used the ballet studios during the day for homeschool theatre, and I started adding as many programs as I could, to try to bring in more revenue. I started choirs, ensembles, preschool music classes, art classes, and group guitar classes. The problem? It didn't work. My focus was split between so many different areas and programs and we just didn't have enough marketing dollars to truly promote and grow every class. I was juggling numbers, spreadsheets, and enrollment numbers—not my sweet spot. This resulted in frustration and even depression. I was doing everything I knew how to do, and it wasn't enough.

In the fall of 2011, I made the radical choice to leave the ballet studio, lease my own commercial space, and solely focus on private lessons. In a way, it was the death of a dream. Having a "Center for the Arts," filled with various classes and programs, was now gone. But what good is a dream that doesn't pay the bills and cover the overhead? I knew this new direction was the right one and I hired a business coach to get me out of the red and on the right track.

At my encouragement, my parents split off into a separate company (which is still growing and thriving today!) and I simplified all our marketing and systems. With laser focus and dedication, I concentrated on filling my location with private music students. It wasn't always easy, and there were moments when I fell to my knees, begging God for wisdom and discernment on what to do next. I stayed on my knees, tears falling down my face, until all my angst was gone, and I could feel peace again. Standing up, straightening my shoulders, I went back to work. Focused and determined, I focused on the big picture while taking the next tiny baby step. My favorite quote became, "Do what you can, with what you have, where you are." That was first said by Teddy Roosevelt when his men desperately needed more ammunition at the battlefront. However, there was no more ammunition to be found. He rallied the troops and encouraged them to keep going. He knew they had to get creative with what they had, or die trying.

2.   Keep your eyes straight ahead

It's difficult, but necessary, to keep your eyes on the mountaintop while taking the next baby step in front of you. Where's the next foothold? What's the next move forward? If you forget where you're going, you'll make a campfire and pitch your tent and stay where you are. But if you determine to keep moving forward—no matter what—then you will eventually reach the summit. Your dreams will come true.

Early on, I knew that I had to multiply myself. The only way to truly grow a company is to invest in staff and not try to do everything all by yourself. However, it's difficult to lead people. People will let you down, leave you for a better opportunity, or simply won't fulfill what they promised they would. Regardless, I pressed on. I had a bigger vision of getting my family out of debt and out from under the weight of living paycheck to paycheck. I knew the potential of our music school. I saw the empty rooms and imagined them filled with teachers and students, making and enjoying music: singing, playing piano, strumming the guitar, swaying with a violin, rocking on the drums. Those dreams became reality because I kept my eyes on a goal bigger than my current circumstances.

Despite the hardships of hiring and training people, I knew I needed staff to help me manage all the details and administration of running a music school. I chose to invest in staff, rather than doing it all by myself. This kept my eyes above the daily details of the school and allowed me to focus on the growth of the company. My success came while focusing on building my team and learning to trust that their gifts and abilities would fill in my weaknesses and make the entire company stronger.

3.   Push Through the Hard Times

Looking back on my journey, I don't think there was one breakthrough moment. My success came largely in my tenacity: my determination to never stop, never quit, and to just keep going.

Just when we were starting to really make some serious headway with our finances, we decided to take another huge risk. I persuaded Chris to quit his job at our church and come home to help me grow the music school full time. It was like we were playing the game of Chutes and Ladders: just when we reached a new level, down the slide we went. We went back to clipping coupons, freezing our spending, pinching pennies, and stretching the food budget. But it worked. With two of us focused on marketing, we could each stick to our strengths: Chris is techy and detail-oriented; I'm creative, a writer, and focused on the big picture. We were astounded with how much less stress we felt with Chris working from home and helping with all the daily tasks for the business and our home. We truly own our own time, and although we must stay very focused and dedicated, we can get a lot more accomplished with both of us working on the business together.

Yes, there have been times of intense conflict and fighting. It's not easy to work with your spouse, but we are determined to make it work, and that's what makes all the difference. If you are focused and determined to reach your goals, you will.

4.   Never Stop Learning

As my company grew, I kept learning new skills as a business owner. I already knew all about music, but suddenly I had to learn about budgeting, marketing, payroll, and laws about contractors and employees. I studied, hired business coaches, attended conferences, and surrounded myself with other successful business owners.

I'll tell you the secret to success: never stop learning. We live in a beautiful age of technology and information. You can learn anything you want to! You simply must have the desire to learn. I homeschool my kids, so this is a lesson I teach them every day: love to learn, know how to learn, and never stop learning.

Along every step of my business, I have invested in my education and it has always been worth every penny spent. Successful people have gone before me, learned from their mistakes, and now want to teach me the lessons they learned. It's truly the fastest way to succeed.

I am a reader, but there are plenty of conferences, podcasts, and video classes available, if reading isn't your preferred learning style. Everyone learns differently and there is no shame if you'd rather listen to an audio book than to read it. Maybe you prefer attending conferences or having lively conversations and discussions. Whichever way you learn best, lean into it. Take a learning style assessment online and never, ever stop learning.

When I started working with my first business coach, I had so many questions and concerns! The first conversation with him was like a gift from heaven. All the swirling questions were laid to rest. He had calm, direct answers for everything I asked, and best of all, he steered me in the right direction. Although I was consumed with questions, I needed to be re-directed in a slightly different direction, for maximum results. As soon as I focused on what he told me to, everything changed. And now it's the same for the business owners that I advise. I give them direction and solutions and they see faster results than if they had kept pushing forward alone.

We all need someone who has gone before us and a light to shine on our path. That's why I love one-on-one coaching. Your investment in learning and knowledge and expert coaching will multiply and grow, if you invest wisely, listen to the advice given, and take action. You can't just keep learning-- you must get out there and apply it.

5. Focus on Your Strengths

As our company has grown, the biggest lesson I have learned is to allow everyone on our team to operate in their sweet spot as much as possible. I am committed to learning the strengths of my team and assigning them responsibilities that match what they are naturally good at doing. Stress comes when we are doing things that go against our natural abilities. I should not work with formulas and spreadsheets. I can do it, but my head threatens to explode and I get frustrated easily. Conversely, it's easy for my husband and numbers energize him. I encourage you to turn up the volume on the things you are good at! What is easy for you? What comes naturally? What's enjoyable for you? Focus on those things. When you are in your unique zone of doing what you were created to do, you will be energized and accomplish more! When you delegate or eliminate the things that drain you and frustrate you, life will be much more enjoyable! If you are growing a company, hire the things that drag you down and focus on your sweet spot. Do what only you can do. Do what you do best!

When I look back over my life, and see how far I have come, I am so thankful for the journey. Every struggle, every tear I cried, and every difficult season we have endured has been worth the sweet taste of reaching our goals, accomplishing our dreams, and helping other people to grow and thrive. I wouldn't trade my journey for an easier path, even if offered one. The hard times have made the good times more beautiful to savor.

We all face adversity in different ways, but the principles to survive and thrive are the same:

1. Choose to rise above

2. Keep your eyes straight ahead

3. Push through the hard times

4. Never stop learning

5. Focus on your strengths

Starting a company with no money, support, or resources, while having four small children at home, gave me the strength and tenacity I need to be successful. The emotional and mental hardships molded me into the person that I am today. I am grateful for the trials, for they were lessons in disguise, teaching me how to be a more patient, loving, giving version of myself.

If you are struggling today, remember that internal strength is just like a muscle of our body: the more we use it, the stronger it becomes. Instead of cursing your trials, look for the silver lining.

Hanging above my fireplace is a wooden sign that says, "There is always, always, always something to be grateful for." In our darkest days, we can fall asleep thankful for our blessings and for the good in our lives. In some ways, my favorite memory is hunting for change to scrape together enough money to go shopping at garage sales. My kids had no idea that our bank account went to zero every month. They just thought we were on a grand adventure, driving through the neighborhood, hunting for free or nearly free toys.

Perspective changes everything. I choose joy in the journey. And that has made all the difference.

About the Author, Jen Hickle

You can find Jen here:
Facebook: www.facebook.com/jenhickle1
Instagram: https://www.instagram.com/jenhickle/
www.neveraloneservices.com

Hickle Enterprises, which brings in nearly a million dollars each year and supports churches, ministries, and missionaries with resources, funds, musical instruments, and printed music, is owned by Chris and Jen Hickle. Jen has authored two books, "Happy Kids, Growing Biz" and "Everything You Need to Know About Music Lessons," and is a consultant to business owners all over the United States, Canada, and in the U.K. Jen works from home and homeschools her four kids in beautiful Minnesota. She is the founder and director of award-winning and nationally famous school, Rogers School of Music, where 450 students take private music lessons each week.

Jen is a community leader and an author, speaker, and business coach. She and her husband have helped start 3 churches. In addition, Jen started Front Porch Musical Theatre, where students of all ages learn to sing, act and dance on stage. She founded a homeschool co-op and runs two community Facebook groups of over 1200 homeschooling moms. Jen thrives on a challenge and loves helping business owners grow their companies by improving their marketing, messaging, and systems. The Hickles love to travel! When they are home, Jen is never too busy for a cup of coffee, a good book, writing, or enjoying time with her friends.

Aligned is the New Hustle

By Rochelle Okoye

Rochelle is a professional Stunt Woman and Actress in the film industry, residing in Vancouver, BC. She is also the co-owner & operator of Tristar Vancouver Martial Arts, in Vancouver, BC.

A ll I've ever known is living a life outside of my comfort zone, from a very young age. So, I guess that was molded into my being and something that definitely helped contribute to the success and where I am today. My whole life, I have competed and worked in industries that are predominately dominated by males. Possessing certain characteristics is a must if one wants to push past the barriers and overcome the adversity one faces on such a path. I have unintentionally inspired others from all walks of lives; both male and female, children and adults, to stand in their power and their courage, to face their demons and to conquer them in order to reach and attain their goals, whatever they may be.

Yes, my career is making movies and providing hard hitting action and drama that entertain the masses. But along the way it has taught me so much more than that. It has taken me to a level of consciousness I was not expecting at the time of embarking on this journey. It has brought me to the highest of highs and also brought me to the lowest of lows. But through it all, I have been forced to sit with my soul, my ego, my heart and myself in order to decipher just what exactly my purpose is and how to go about fulfilling it.

Being a female co-owner of Tristar Vancouver Martial Arts has entailed overcoming adversity for more than one reason. To be honest, it has been an endeavour that at times I thought I could not endure or follow through with wholeheartedly or completely. Originally, I co-owned the business with two men, one of whom I was also in an abusive relationship with. This proved to elicit more challenges than I could ever foresee coming. I was faced with toxic, abusive projections of inner demons that I had no choice but to deal with at the time, as they were hurled in hurricane force towards me and my business, with no compassion and no empathy from my abuser. Through his lies, betrayal, deceit, manipulation, cheating, abuse of many forms, stealing and harassment, I was pushed down to some of my saddest, lowest and darkest days. I chose to pick myself up from the darkness and work through the painful storm so that I may see the sun shine again with love and light.

I had no choice but to operate and run our successful MMA gym, work my stunt and acting career, while also healing from the trauma and abuse my now, ex-boyfriend and now, ex-business partner had bestowed upon me. It was a painful, trying and extremely exhausting time in my life. After the professional and legal decision was made to remove this partner from the business, the continual projections of toxic behaviour and inner demons continued to be hurled towards me, my business and the other business partner both publicly and privately. Through it all though, I have continued to try my best to rise above the hurt, the negativity and to heal from it, to forgive and to understand that we are all on our own journeys and paths. I truly believe, only hurt people go out of their way to hurt other people, especially hurting loved ones. For a grown man to bully and abuse a woman of any sort, is a man who clearly needs healing and love.

My journey is to continue to heal from what was projected onto me, so that I may continue moving forward with love, light, strength, courage and forgiveness in my heart. Creating a continual, free flowing, loving and open space in the core of myself for me is so important in order to heal and to let go. It has not been an easy road to healing by any means. In a situation such as this, it takes time and I understand that time and love heals all wounds. I have had some highs and a lot of lows along the way. But whenever I hit a low and feel like I can't continue on because of the residual damage created, I open my heart to remembering all the reasons why I opened the gym to begin with. To be able to help others to achieve and attain their own personal and career goals is an invaluable lesson and gift one can provide for someone else and the universe collectively as a whole. I have worked extremely hard to be in the position I am in today, but I count my blessings daily because of it and I carry a sense of gratitude that keeps a smile on my face and a world of abundance free flowing through my heart no matter the situation.

My current business partner, Kajan Johnson, is also my best friend, coach, highly skilled veteran and mixed martial artist who currently fights in the UFC. We continue to thrive and rise above all the adversity we have been faced with. We have managed to provide a positive, fun, loving environment & facility where other martial artists can come and learn from one of the best in the country. Not only to learn physical skills but it's also a place where people can collectively learn and evolve consciously. It's the national training centre for the Canadian National Mixed Martial Arts team and training centre for multiple top level athletes, stunt performers, actors, and television and film productions. We welcome everyone from all walks of life with all levels of skill and abilities. Together, we truly look forward to continuing growing our business and the Tristar Vancouver Family. Kajan and I both feel extremely grateful to be able to provide a business that helps serve all to their highest good. The gym has become such a positive environment and walking into the facility, you can just feel the vast amount of loving, and happy energy flowing through it. It really is such a beautiful thing to witness and experience. The team is succeeding as a whole, we're family. New members are pouring in daily and loving the training, the environment, the coaching and the dynamic of the team. It really is such a blessing to be a part of. Team work truly makes the dream work and I'm grateful for each and everyone one of our members and fighters on our team. The sky is the limit. Life will give you whatever experience is the most helpful for the evolution of your consciousness, both good and bad. And this whole experience has only made me stronger, wiser, more courageous, loving and vulnerable.

The Adversity

Becoming a stuntwoman, actress and owner of a mixed martial arts gym was never something on my radar or life/career goals growing up. In fact, when I was growing up I wasn't really sure what I wanted to do. It goes back to the whole philosophy of flowing, and one thing leading to the next. One door closing and deciding to have courage to embark on whatever the universe presents and opens to you next.

Growing up, I was a gymnast on the Great Britain Gymnastic Team. I was a 2000 Olympic hopeful and 3x National champion. I retired from gymnastics when I was 15 years old after the eligibility rules changed and I was told I would have to wait until the 2004 Olympics to compete. My parents, siblings and I moved back to Canada, where I was born. My parents had high hopes that I would carry on my athletic endeavors with gymnastics and compete for the Canadian National team in the 2004 Olympics; I had other hopes and aspirations.

My parents pressured me quite intensely and consistently throughout the next year to make my return to gymnastics. They found it necessary to continually bring up the fact that I had accomplished so much at such a young age, and my talents were just going to waste. How could I not regret this? But gymnastics wasn't something I really enjoyed doing. It was something I happened to be extremely good at, but the passion and desire within my soul for it never existed.

Growing up in my household wasn't your average first world family experience. There were many incidents and situations that should have never taken place. My siblings and I endured a challenging lifetime of physical, emotional, mental and verbal abuse from my parents. My biological immediate family is broken and torn. My father disowned my two siblings and I 12 years ago when I was 21 years old. We are currently estranged and have been since that day, however my mother and father are currently still together and married. My siblings and myself are also currently estranged, something I continually hope will change in the near future.

Growing up, my father always wanted me to take the academia route with education and career. He chose what I was to do with my life, before I was even born; an international Olympic level gymnast/pro athlete and a lawyer or doctor to follow. Some say I would have made an amazing lawyer, but that does not fall in my calling or passion.

After I retired from gymnastics and moved back to Canada, I manage to skip a grade and graduate high school a year early at 16 years old. I enrolled in University when I was 17 yrs. old and graduated with my degree on my 21st birthday. Of course, my father wanted me to go into law and pursue a career in that field, but I informed him I wished to pursue a degree in psychology. I was always the kid everyone came to for advice, and I was always the person everyone and anyone would approach and unload all their personal and most private issues and problems onto. I guess I've always been that person that people tend to feel comfortable opening up to and expressing anything. I have always been an empath, I have always felt a lot in life and I have always been extremely intuitive and communicative. All of which have been natural blessings and gifts given to me from childhood or birth. Psychology resonated with me more than anything else at the time. I knew I had to have a deeper understanding of the level of abuse I had endured during childhood, and I knew I had to heal from it. I knew from a young age that it was my duty to stop the intergenerational cycle of abuse in my family; I took that responsibility on myself. I intuitively knew a lot of things at a young age that ended up happening in my adult future.

I went to university, completed my degree in psychology, I studied psychopathy and behavioral psychology specifically. I gained a better understanding into the issues of my mother and father and the abuse they projected onto myself and my siblings growing up. I was able to start my healing journey, coming from a place of love, empathy, and forgiveness. This did not happen overnight, it took 7 years from that point forward and a lot more adversity, hardship, challenges, losses, and lessons learned to close the chapter and accept the fact I have and will continue to walk through life without the loving help and support of parents.

Growing up I never heard the words, "I love you," from my father. Not even once, no kisses, not one hug that I can recall, and it was extremely awkward and uncomfortable and limited to zero affection. He supported us academically and in our athletic careers, but that's as far as the love and support would extend. My siblings and I lived in terror and fear of my father. The abuse was a daily thing. Not only did we experience it amongst ourselves, we had to witness each other go through it and witness my father verbally and emotionally abusing my mother. I had no bond and no attachment to my parents, so much so that when I asked if I was adopted, my mother often times replied with yes. I had always felt since I could remember, that I didn't belong here or with them, as weird as this sounds, I always felt as if aliens had dropped me off on this planet and for whatever reason my parents happened to stumble upon me and find me. I realize now, that feeling results from the lack of love from the 2 most important people on this earth plane, your parents. As part of the human experience, two specific people, who have navigated it before us, for a reason, bring us into this enormous, terrifying world. And when that support system doesn't exist and that unconditional love is not provided, it can lead to a world of chaos for an individual as they try to navigate their place on this earth on their own. They have to try and learn everything on their own. It can make for very frightening times, if a person doesn't possess the strong spirit to do whatever they need to do to better themselves and figure it out with love for themselves.

Throughout my experiences and my healing journey, I've come to learn and empathize that my mother is just a broken soul, trapped in a tower with a key, but without the strength or the courage to unlock the door and save herself. It's the result and behavioral pattern from the many years of abuse she's endured from my father and for whatever reason she does not possess the character or the love for herself and her own soul to do what she needs to do to free herself and reestablish a relationship with her children. I promised myself as a child that I would be the opposite of my parents. I promised myself that I would strive every day to not be like them. And to learn from them on the deepest level. I knew at a young age that would require a lot of work, and that my path was not going to be easy by any means, but I was determined and I have always possessed a warrior spirit, something my father also helped nurture through his violent and abusive ways.

My upbringing was extremely militant. My father was a child soldier in the Biafra war, in Nigeria. One can only imagine the trauma and suffering he experienced and saw with his very own young eyes. He was clearly affected by trauma that he chose to never heal from in his adulthood. He moved to Manitoba as a young man and met my mother in Winnipeg, where they married and had 3 kids. Growing up with a father that is a psychopath and overcoming the challenges of that has molded me into the person I am today, it's also provided many lessons and blessings.

Throughout my upbringing, my siblings and I endured odd forms of punishment and abuse whenever my father saw fit. Most of the time it was about nothing, simply a projection of his own inner demons and hurts he refused to face in his lifetime. We were not allowed to react to the abuse or show any form of emotion other than stone face. If my sibling or I were to cry because of the inflicted pain the punishment elicited, we were punished harder and called, "Weak!" We were forced and taught to be strong, through pain and suffering.

As part of his technique to control and mold, my siblings and I lived life on a schedule that my father had written out pertaining to each of our own needs, down to the very minute. If I didn't follow my schedule, punishment was enforced. My daily regimen looked something like this: I would go to school for the day, come home and eat a snack quickly and get ready for gym between 3:30-4:30pm. 5pm gymnastics starts, finish at 9pm. Go home to finish homework and eat dinner and go to bed for 10:30/11pm. Wake up and do it again. I trained 6-7x a week in gymnastics. Mostly 6 days a week for 4 hours a day. When I was at the national training center I would train 8-9 hours a day, 6 days a week, and we missed a week of school. So overall training consisted of 30-40 hours a week. It was a lot for a child to go through, I had no childhood and zero social life. Combined with not really loving the sport, but just too good at it to quit, I was not enjoying my life at this period in time.

If we failed our chores or missed something, physical abuse was the punishment. If we didn't ask for something before taking it – punished. If we did not reply with, "Yes sir" or "No sir" – punished. If we did not say good morning or good night to our father – punished. If we took a sip of juice from the fridge without asking – punished. He would always know if juice was missing because he would measure it and mark lines on the container. Bad grades, punished, step out of line, punished, everything was punishment and abuse. Sometimes my father would yell so loud at us, we couldn't even understand the words that were coming out of his mouth. Sometimes, the abuse and the punishment we endured was so intense, my older brother would faint or vomit in anticipation of the abuse he was about to endure. Of course, when he awoke, he would be called weak, or useless or put down in some awful way by my father.

In 2006, I attained my bachelor of science in psychology from the University of British Columbia. I relocated back to Vancouver, where my parents resided. In June 2006, after my graduation and return home to Vancouver, my parents decided that I was out of the family and they officially disowned me. My father had always told me we had 3 strikes and then we're out.

My first strike occurred when social services were involved in our home life when I was 15 in high school due to the abuse my father was inflicting. I had a panic attack at school and didn't want to go home. Of course, I was brought into the counselor's office, where they asked me questions and then the authorities got involved. Later, my mother made me apologize to my father for the abuse he inflicted on us and for not being strong enough to handle it.

My second strike was when I graduated from University. It was my birthday and graduation day, a day that should have been filled with many blessings and a lot of love and celebrations. However, the week before, my father wanted me to follow his orders and allow him to get me a job. I am very independent and have been since a young age, as I wasn't able to rely on my parents for much, including finances. I had put myself through University, with student loans, part time work, while going to school full time and my parents controlled my student loan money by allotting me a specific amount each week to live off of and then keeping some for themselves. All of which I paid back myself. I managed to find myself my own job, of course, as I wanted nothing for my father to hold over my head anymore and control me by. So I did exactly that, which he of course was opposed to and enraged by. He knew the minute I started doing things my way and for myself would be the day he loses all power and control over me which would be his downfall and demise of his existence in his reality. During that particular phone conversation, he called me numerous awful names, and continued to be extremely condescending and belittle me, something he was very good at. He then hung up on me. My mother proceeded to call me back and of course take his side, asking, "Why can't you reply with 'Yes, sir' or 'No, Sir'?" adding that I should know better by now. Honestly, at the time I was still only 20 years old, but I thought I was so much more grown up. I had had enough of their abuse, and I had learned so much about trauma and psychological issues through attaining my degree, that my soul would no longer allow my abusers to abuse me like this anymore. I had to stand up for myself; I had to stand in my power. So, for the first time I did. I told her that I do not appreciate their abuse. I told them how wrong and toxic it is, how lost they are and how they need to find themselves and face their demons and conquer their issues. How abusing your children on such an extreme level is wrong and only sets the child up for more issues and problems in their future and they will carry on the cycle of abuse to their children. To this, my mother replied by mocking me and putting me down in the most immature, hurtful way possible. To which I decided the most loving thing I could do for myself in that moment was to hang up the phone. And so I did. Little did I know then, that that moment would be a defining point for the strength and courage I would have to keep demonstrating in order to save my own life.

My third and final strike happened when I returned from University, on Father's Day. My father called me over, as he was unhappy with the events that unfolded the week prior, which happened to be my university graduation and birthday. My parents had informed me they were not going to show up to and support me because of the phone call argument that happened earlier. It turns out that they did attend my graduation, but not to my knowledge. I literally just found them there at my ceremony and it was extremely uncomfortable, awkward and hurtful to say the least. I didn't receive one congratulations and not one happy birthday. The only thing my father had to say to me when he found me at the end of my commencement was, "You think life is difficult now? Just wait!"

Fast forward 1 week later, I am now sitting at his house with my mother on the couch about to embark on 3 hour family meeting, which means 3 hours of extreme abuse that one must endure. In this meeting, my father was extremely upset and angry that I chose to attain a career on my own. He yelled at me for 3 hours and tried to make me feel small and timid like a scared puppy as he always does. All of which I was not having and for the first time in my life, I decided to speak up for myself to him in person, and not take this on anymore. I chose something different for me. I chose to stand in my power against him. I chose to be my own superhero and that's exactly what I did. He responded with violence, as he could not tolerate his daughter, 20 years younger than him, and female, standing up for herself against a man, an abuser, her father, an elder. Instead of hitting me at that moment, which I was fully prepared to receive, he ran to the bathroom and in a fit of fury he proceeded to punch holes in the wall. I got up and said that's my queue to leave. I ran down the stairs to the front door and on the way out my mother yelled, "Thanks a lot Rochelle!" That was the last time I saw my mother and father. After I left, they called me and told me I am officially out of the family. That I am on my own, that I am weak and wild and out of control, undeserving of love and family, protection and support and that I am officially disowned.

Moving Into the Positive

The day my parents disowned me was the day my life began and changed for the better. It was an extremely painful and terrifying blessing in disguise.

Without the overbearing control, abuse and the fear of my parents, I knew I was now free to do whatever my heart desired. I now could live life for me, and embark on what I was meant to do on this earth plane this time around. So I began exploring my passions and what made me vibrate the highest. I worked in my field of psychology for 2 years counseling children with developmental disabilities and behavioral problems. It was such a rewarding job and a stepping-stone to becoming a family and marital therapist, which is what I thought I wanted to do at the time. I applied to grad school and got in, but something was missing. I still didn't feel complete. I was missing athletics and sports and competition and the challenges and growth it can provide. So I started boxing recreationally, which eventually turned serious. Boxing provided a healthy outlet for me and some healing surrounding my physically abusive upbringing. And it wasn't long before I started fighting as an amateur and then I went pro.

I fell into my stunt and acting career through my fight career. At the time I had no idea one thing was leading me to the next and had been my entire life. While still embarking on my professional fight career, a stunt-acting role came up in the film world; the character was a kick boxer. One of my really good friends and stunt men, Paul Lazenby, who also happened to be my ring announcer for my last pro fight, suggested I audition for the role and look into a career in film. He introduced me to my now really good friend, James Bamford (Bam Bam), who was the stunt coordinator and now is a director and producer for CW's, Arrow. Bam Bam took me under his wing and showed the ropes and then set me free to soar and fly on my own. I networked and met other professionals in the industry and brought what I could to the table, which seemed to be appreciated and looked upon with excitement and gratitude, which of course made me feel like this is meant to be and in return I felt extremely grateful and blessed. Everything took off so quickly. I realized, in that moment, everything I had worked so hard towards had put me here. Without a high-level career in gymnastics and boxing, I simply would not possess the skill or talent that is appreciated and respected in my line of work. I would not be where I am right now.

So there I was, a young woman at the age of 25, in a new career, with little to no support, terrified of all the changes and everything this career encompasses. It is not for the weak at all. In fact, this career weeds out the weak pretty fast. But I believed in myself and I knew if this is what I wanted to do then I would have to give it my all and put everything I can into it, and that's exactly what I did. I went into my film career full force blazing trails. I ended up booking big roles in big features and television shows immediately, all of which I was so extremely grateful for. Here I am 7 years later, still going a strong, coming back from a near career-ending injury, being able to maintain and continue to grow my career in film and just so extremely grateful for it all. I am currently working on Xmen: Dark Phoenix (my 3rd movie in the franchise) as Storm's stunt double. I have now completed acting, stunt doubling and stunting in over 100 other major motion feature films and network television shows (http://www.imdb.com/name/nm3876369/?ref_=fn_al_nm_1).

As the Co-owner of a successful mixed Martials arts gym, I feel extremely blessed and grateful for the empire I have managed to build and continue to grow every day. I was thrown to the wolves and forced to figure it out on my own, literally sink or swim; even if I'm drowning, I will figure out how to swim and make it to shore. I have been fighting battles my whole life. I am not a survivor, I am a warrior. I prayed every day to manifest the people I needed in my life to help guide me along the way, and they appeared, and when they appeared I listened to what they had to say and I executed. And that is the secret formula. It's one thing to ask the universe for what you want, but you also have to put in the work and show the universe your vibrations, show the universe that this is what you want, and you're willing to take risks to succeed at it. Follow this recipe and the universe will respond. It is the universal law.

Growing up with extremely abusive parents has been my blessing in disguise. Rumi quotes it best: Both light and shadow are the dance of love. You cannot have one without the other. It's that simple. We must grow through what we go through, bad happens so that good can come. We make mistakes and fall on our faces so that we can pick ourselves up, learn, evolve, grow and give back. For that is the whole purpose of this life. To learn unconditional love and to apply it to ourselves as well as to one another. If I hadn't struggled, if I hadn't had parents that did not support me or love me or abuse me or abandon and leave me for dead, I would not have embarked on my healing journey to heal my heart, my soul, my trauma. I would not have a Bachelors of Science degree in psychology. I would not have helped all those children I counseled who desperately needed love and support in their lives. I would not have had the courage and the strength to stand on my own two feet and go after what I want in life. What is meant for me? If I did not face and overcome my adversity, I would not possess any of the characteristics it takes for a person to succeed and to give back.

From the day my parents disowned me, until now, I have not stopped my healing journey. Every day is an opportunity to grow and become a better version of myself. Healing for me comes in many forms; I always count my blessings and express what I'm grateful for, at least 5 things a day. I journal a lot, and am extremely mindful of the words I use to talk to myself and describe myself. I try to put out as much love and kindness into the world so that it may be reciprocated. I spend a lot of time in nature, as I'm very sensitive and an empath, it is so important, especially for me to reset my vibrational frequency. I don't watch a lot of TV and I try not to listen or pay attention to things that cause a low vibrational frequency, such as propaganda, processed foods, chemicals, violence on TV, war, toxic people etc. I eat organic and all natural food, I drink a lot of tea and water, I try not to poison my body; I view it as a temple, and it's sacred. I am very careful with who I exchange energy with and bring into my circle. I physically exercise, of course every day, and I really just try to do things that I enjoy doing. I volunteer and give back and I try to always be there for people no matter how I'm feeling. I tap into higher self and God and the universe. It's important to embark on a spiritual journey, whatever that may look like for you. As long as you are connecting to something higher outside of yourself and within yourself you will find the answers you seek when sitting in silence. It's my motto in life to walk with love in your heart no matter what you go through.

I think it's also important to note and truly understand that all human emotion is normal, and it's important to feel it all, it's a part of healing and growing. Sadness and anger is just as much a part of healing and growth as inner peace and happiness. One must feel the low in order to feel the high and vice versa. I believe a lot of new age enlightenment material confuses readers with this quite a bit. People often look at my life and only see the positive. They forget that all those who have succeeded before me and all those after me have also had the ability to overcome adversity, disappointment and even tragedy in their lives. I have been depressed, I have been down and out, and I have fallen on my face and thought I would never ever be able to get back up, just like everybody else. I have had days where all I can do is cry, where I have felt so alone and exhausted. And even on those days, even if I don't feel it the moment and it comes to me the next day, I am proud of myself for feeling all of it. Enduring the storm and the lows, is all a part of healing and the journey, it shows strength, it builds character. How long you stay with those emotions and what you do with them is what truly matters. Recognize the emotion, acknowledge and respect it and then when it has served its purpose in your life, release it and let it go and thank it for coming. Honor it. Just like Buddha said, "Your mind is everything, what you think, you become." I lived by this after my parents disowned me and it has taken me very far. So be kind to yourself, be gentle and be love.

Remember when I said, grow through what you go through and don't let it make you bitter or angry? This is so important. And this is where I hear a lot of people struggle. It is so easy to make excuses for our poor behavior in life. It is so easy to turn a blind eye to the hurt you may have caused somebody. It is so easy to ignore the person standing next to you. But why be like that? Being the opposite will make you feel better internally. Taking responsibility for our issues, for our demons whether or not someone else helped contribute to them, is the first and most important key to healing. Take responsibility for your own life. Yes, it might make you feel uncomfortable at first, it might make you feel bad, or guilty or wrong, but the pay off in the long run is undeniably much higher for your soul, for all of humanity. Your particular circumstances can make or break you in life. You decide. Be the victim or the victor. I choose to be my own super hero every day! I choose to be the victor. We all have that choice. I owe that to myself and to God, to the universe and to others. Collectively we are one, and the more people that love and work on themselves, the better our planet and collective level of consciousness is as a whole.

That being said, I am so extremely grateful for the hardship, challenges and abuse my parents bestowed upon me and for all the other adversity not mentioned in this chapter that I have had to face and overcome on my own. Without it, I simply would not be who I am today. And I can honestly look at myself in the mirror and proudly say, "I love Rochelle Okoye and I am so proud of the woman you have become." I hope that we can all share that ability, that authenticity and love for ourselves and for one another. So the next time you're feeling down and times are tough and the whole world feels like it's going against you, remember that the airplane always takes off against the wind, not with it. Strength does not come from winning; your struggles develop your strengths. When you go through hardships and decide not to surrender, that is strength. Just decide that you want it more than you are afraid of it and you will succeed regardless of the outcome and always be love no matter what.

About the Author, Rochelle Okoye

Instagram: @rochelle_okoye
Facebook: Rochelle Okoye
Twitter: @rochelleokoye
IMDB:
http://www.imdb.com/name/nm3876369/?ref_=fn_al_nm_1
Website: www.tristarvancouver.com
Instagram: @tristar_vancouver
Twitter: @tristar_vancity
Facebook Page: Tristar Vancouver Martial Arts Inc.
(@tristarvancouver)

Rochelle was born in Winnipeg, Manitoba and began her gymnastics career at the very early age of 2. When Rochelle was 7 yrs. old, both her parents decided to uproot the family and move to Leeds,

England, where her father finished his PhD at Cambridge and Oxford University.

Rochelle continued her gymnastics career and at the age of 9, became a member of and competed internationally for the Great Britain Gymnastics Team. In 1996, Rochelle became the Great Britain National Gymnastics Champion and retained the title for 3 consecutive years.

Rochelle was also nominated and awarded 'The Top Sports Person in England under the age of 13 category,' for 2 consecutive years. At the age of 14, BBC produced and aired a one hour documentary called 'Going for Gold,' focusing primarily on her goals of competing in the 2000 Olympics. Unfortunately, her dreams fell short when the International Gymnastics Federation (FGI) announced that a competitor must now be 16 years of age to compete in the Olympics. Rochelle was turning 15, and sadly, was one year shy of being eligible to qualify.

With the Olympics another 4 years out of her reach, her family decided the best thing to do was pack it in and return to Canada, in the hopes that Rochelle would continue her career on the Canadian team. She however had other plans. She resigned from gymnastics, focused on her studies and graduated from Terry Fox High School a year early at the age of 16.

In 2006 and only 20 yrs. old, she graduated with a B.Sc. in Psychology from the University of Northern British Columbia. She worked in her field for 2 years, counseling and working one-on-one with children with developmental disabilities, mental illnesses and behavioral problems. Although a very rewarding job, she did not feel completely fulfilled. She decided it was time to return to the world of sports.

Rochelle started training and competing in Amateur and Professional Boxing, Brazilian Jiu Jitsu and Muay Thai. She had her first amateur boxing fight after 6 months of training and made the decision with her coach, Tony Pep to go pro after only 1 year. She made her pro debut in 2008 at the Red Robinson Show Theatre in Coquitlam, BC, where she won by unanimous decision and went down in history alongside opponent, Priscilla Trampowsky as the first professional female boxers to have fought in BC.

On the pursuit of helping others achieve their fitness goals, Rochelle also attained her personal training degree and started coaching, personal training and running fitness boot camps. Rochelle is currently the co-owner of one of Canada's most prestigious mixed martial training facility, Tristar Vancouver Martial Arts, located in Vancouver BC. Where she co owns and operates the gym with her business partner Kajan Johnson who currently fights in the UFC. Tristar Vancouver also happens to be the National Training Centre for The Canadian National MMA team.

After embarking on all of her athletic endeavors and education, Rochelle made a guided decision to jump full force into the film industry. Using all of her talents and skills acquired along the way, she travels all over the world filming and making some of Hollywood's biggest movies and TV shows. She now has a 7-year successful career as a Stunt Woman and Actress working alongside some of Hollywood's biggest names on the some of Hollywood's biggest major motion feature films and Television Network shows.

Rochelle is currently also in the works of writing a memoire based on her life experiences and 4 guide books on overcoming adversity and choosing success in different aspects and areas of life. Her goal is to have the books consecutively published throughout the next year to come and will be touring and public speaking. She will be available for bookings through her agent and website.

Take Courage to Stand

By Lauretha Ward

When we go through periods of suffering, trials, and pain it is not just for us to go through with the intent of wandering around or staying in our wilderness experience. Yes, I know this is easier said than done, but when suffering it helps to rest and stand on God's promise, knowing that the difficult season will pass. I realize that as believers we all love the part about being qualified as heirs of God and fellow heirs with Christ as partakers of His spiritual blessing and inheritance. But along with this, we must also share in His suffering, as this is how we become stronger and powerful in Him. We endure our tests and come through with testimonies to share with others as to how we become overcomers. Having gone through a trial victoriously brings comfort and strength to others and glory to God. And if [we are His] children, [then we are His] heirs also: heirs of God and fellow heirs with Christ [sharing His spiritual blessing and inheritance], if indeed we share in His suffering so that we may also share in His glory (Romans 8:17, AMP).

I've gone through numerous trials in which I had to walk the talk with putting my spiritual weapons of prayer, fasting, and praising God into action. I understand that physicians practice medicine based upon medical training they have received. Though many of them are not believers, the knowledge they gained still comes from God whether they believe in Him or not. Therefore, there is nothing that can supersede the miraculous power of the Lord, our Great Physician. The matter has been settled for the Bible says …and with the stripes [that wounded] Him we are healed and made whole (Isaiah 53: 5, AMP). It doesn't say we will be healed. It says we are healed because of the finished work on the cross. So that means that the outcome of what I experienced in February 2006 was set from the beginning---"And with the stripes that wounded Him I am healed and made whole"--- I can honestly tell you that this Scripture was the furthest thing from my mind as I was going through pain at that time.

In February 2006, I had developed shortness of breath, a chronic cough, wheeze, and fever. I went to the doctor to get some medicine so I could return to work quickly. At first I began taking the medicine for influenza for about two weeks, but that didn't help. I then was placed on medication for bronchitis. However, that didn't work either and my condition grew worse. The doctor couldn't nail down a diagnosis and had to try a variety of medicines. "I am a general practitioner, and I am testing different things to see what is going to work for you," is what he told me.

During that unimaginable situation, being confined to the upper level of my home, my husband Gary, and my boys did the best they could to take care of me. I had always been strong, healthy, independent, and vibrant. But I was reduced to someone waiting on me hand and foot because I would get winded going up and down the stairs. Gary and my sons were very loving and patient, bringing me anything that I needed. However, I had a difficult time accepting being flat on my back. I tried different medications and nebulizers but instead of improving, I regressed.

After I had my fill of not getting results from this doctor, I pulled all of my medical records and started doing some research. I then went to a pulmonologist (a doctor specializing in respiratory diseases) seeking a solution. She was going to prescribe the steroid Prednisone for an incurable disease called sarcoidosis. But I refused to accept her diagnosis and told her, "I don't have that". I knew not to claim that illness as mine. Besides, that was just the latest diagnosis I received among the others such as lymphadenopathy and interstitial disease. Because I wouldn't accept that report, I only discussed this with my immediate family, my pastor, and his wife in terms of the symptoms that were present.

So why did I take the medication? I was looking for a quick fix to be able to return to work. When I asked her about the side effects what jumped out at me was weight gain and osteoarthritis. I couldn't imagine putting weight on my 5 foot 2-inch frame. So I compromised and told her that I would take the medicine every other day.

Spiritually speaking, do you realize the devil comes in many forms? It's not always about tempting you to commit adultery or sins of that nature. The devil tries to get you to doubt God. Let me be clear, I am not saying that the doctor is a devil. However, I am saying that the devil comes to kill, steal, and destroy, and he was looking to take me out---if not through sickness, then through the medicine with all of its terrible side effects. God allowed me to see I was under a spiritual attack. We are not ignorant to the devil's devices. The enemy uses incurable diseases as a tactic to bring destruction.

Now, I really could identify with the woman who had an issue of blood twelve years. And who had endured much suffering under [the hands of] many physicians and had spent all that she had, and was no better but instead grew worse (St. Mark 5:26, AMP). I thank God that it was only after giving a testimony at church on the power of prayer and fasting that I eventually came to myself.

I had testified that my oldest son Aaron was diagnosed with the symptoms of asthma and the doctor wanted him to be on the steroid Albuterol. The doctors were telling me that he had asthma and would probably have to receive breathing treatments indefinitely. After having listened to healing scriptures by Pastor Kenneth E. Hagin on tape over and over again, there was no doubt and I believed my son was healed of asthma---so much so, that I decided to go on a three-day Esther fast (no food or water for three days and three nights).

I had faith that God had healed my son, so I put away the breathing machine when I got home after a Friday night Watch Service. I released my faith by an action. For according to James, So also faith, if it does not have works (deeds and actions of obedience to back it up), by itself is destitute of power (inoperative, dead). But someone will say [to you then], You [say you] have faith, and I have [good] works. Now you show me your [alleged] faith apart from any [good] works [if you can], and I by [good] works [of obedience] will show you my faith (James 2:17-18, AMP).

I took action. The spiritual medicine that Aaron began to take every day was this: "Thank you Jesus, that by your stripes I am healed." I'm not going to say that it was easy going through the challenge of hearing the wheezes. But I held onto and declared aloud the truth of God's word in spite of what I was seeing. The symptoms would flare up, however, it began to regress. Aaron to this day doesn't remember ever having the symptom of asthma. I didn't want my son having to take steroids for the rest of his life. God gets all of the glory for healing my son, and I have had many opportunities to share with others the power of God to deliver through prayer and fasting.

On one occasion, when my youngest son Laurence was a newborn, I took him to the doctor for a routine check-up. It was during this visit that the doctor diagnosed him with a heart murmur. Well my mind immediately went back to what God had done with Aaron. I asked God what should I do? He led me to do a five-day liquid fast to believe Him for total healing. During the fast, I anointed and prayed over Laurence. During the next appointment, the doctor examined Laurence and could find no evidence of a heart murmur. My sons are seventeen and twenty-two now, and both have been healthy to this day with the exception of a seasonal cold or flu-like symptoms. I've shared these testimonies in detail along with many others to encourage readers to never lose hope in the most difficult time of your lives in, "Resting On His Promises: I Am Covered from A to Z."

He Did it Before – He Can Do it Again

So now fast forward to me having shared these powerful healing testimonials with the congregation at my church, I began to walk to my seat and the Holy Spirit said to me as I returned to my seat, "Since you believed that I could heal your sons, can you believe that I can heal you?" WOW, this indeed hit me like a bolt of lightning. Wait a minute; I know I'm not in the boat all by myself. Why is it that we can always believe God so strongly for other people? Yet when it comes to praying and trusting that God can come through for us we waver. I had to stop and realize from the testimonials of healing for my sons that if God did it before then He is well able to do it again. He miraculously healed both of my sons of generational curses that were passed down from each side of my family, with asthma on my dad's side of the family and heart murmurs on my mom's side of the family. Those curses were cut off once and for all! So as I sat down in my seat and really listened to the words that I said about the power of God to heal, I realized I had to believe that God would do it for me.

In addition, I heeded the voice of the Lord to tell no one about me stopping my prescribed medication. With having taken only three tablets, I put the bottle away. I felt in my heart that if I continued taking the medicine and was overtaken with side-effects, it would start a vicious cycle of taking medication to continually cure the side-effects. Later the same day I was reading a devotional that included this passage of Scripture: St. Matthew 9:28-30 (AMP) says, When He had reached the house and went in, the blind men came to Him, and Jesus said to them, Do you believe that I am able to do this? They said to Him, Yes, Lord. Then He touched their eyes, saying, According to your faith and trust and reliance [on the power invested in Me] be it done to you; And their eyes were opened. Jesus earnestly and sternly charged them, See that you let no one know about this.

This was a faith walk that I was supposed to do alone. That meant I wasn't to share anything about what I was going to do with my husband, my parents, or my pastor. Like the woman who had an issue of blood I too had to press into Jesus. I decided that I was not going to focus on the problem. I knew that would only hinder my victory. See, the enemy wants us to look at the symptoms, the diagnosis, the prognosis, and the test results. But maintaining focus on the problem would only make the issue bigger. It matters how you see yourself in the midst of experiencing pain. As I spoke aloud the Word I saw myself pain-free. I saw myself breathing normally without wheezing. I saw myself standing in front of the congregation giving a testimony of God healing me in the midst of my suffering. So you have to see yourself well right now! If all you see in your days ahead is being sick and on medication for the rest of your life, then you'll never get well. What you look at and focus on you will begin to empower. Look at the Word of God and believe what He says about healing. Tell yourself that this is just a temporary medical setback. Rather than looking at the symptoms begin to see Jesus as your solution. See yourself symptom-free, pain-free, and disease-free. For she kept saying, If I only touch His garments, I shall be restored to health. And immediately her flow of blood was dried up at the source, and [suddenly] she felt in her body that she was healed of her [distressing] ailment (St. Mark 5:28-29, AMP).

Maintain Possession of Your Confession

In March 2006, I began a 21-day liquid fast because I wanted to rid my body of all toxins from the medication that I had in my system and believe God for divine healing. I followed a daily regimen of speaking "healing scriptures" throughout the day along with singing praise and worship songs. My favorite passage to meditate on was from Jeremiah 17:14, which reads, heal me, O Lord, and I shall be healed; save me, and I shall be saved; for thou art my praise. Faith without works is dead and to put what God was doing in my life to a test, my mom called me and after we had prayed together gave me a word of encouragement and shared that I should go to the basement to praise the Lord. I took heed to the instructions and went down two flights of stairs and gave God a radical praise as a shout unto the Lord with a voice of triumph. There is power in praise! In the middle of life challenges, praising God is a way of releasing faith for the manifestation of your healing. You might be experiencing pain in your body, but if you have a song in your heart, and you began to praise God, your faith is working and watch the shift that will take place in your life. You see praising God will take your mind off of your condition and places it on your Savior, the Great Physician. We can praise God in the midst of adversities knowing that He is behind the scenes working things out for our good. Praise can bring forth the healing needed in your body. Psalm 23:3 reads, God inhabits the praises of His people. Praise is a form of spiritual warfare that brings God's presence into your situation. When I returned to the upper level I was no longer short of breath. Hallelujah! I began to feel stronger and could go up and down stairs in my household without becoming winded. Not long after that, my mom and I began doing 4-mile walks. I then returned back to work in April 2006. Thank God that I too was made whole, as the Great Physician healed my body. Many hardships and perplexing circumstances confront the righteous, but the LORD rescues him from them all. (Psalm 34:19, AMP).

So what happened when I returned back to the pulmonologist in June 2006? The pulmonologist took a look at my chest x-rays and my breathing level had dramatically changed for the better and she couldn't believe the improvement. My blood pressure reading was 114/72, pulse ox was 100/56, and I was 16 pounds lighter. She stated, "Lauretha what did you do, it looks like we can taper the dose for the Prednisone?" I mentioned to her that I fasted, prayed, did holistic treatments of natural herbs, rested, and exercised. Her ears perked up to question "what type of herbs did you take?" I shared with her the natural herbs that I took and of course she didn't ask anything further about my spiritual remedy. She gave me a prescription to continue the Prednisone medication that I immediately discarded when I went out the door, never to return.

I continue to see the pulmonologist in my travels because we treat patients together on a professional basis. I knew that the Lord healed me on day one and I just waited on the manifestation. I thank and praise and give Glory to God for being my Great Physician.

I am an Overcomer

So, why did I go through this particular test? You see, every time I come under a physical attack it gives me the opportunity to stand boldly on the Word of God. I'm then able to declare through Christ Jesus that I am victorious and that God causes me to always triumph. Revelation 12:11, AMP says, And they have overcome (conquered) him (devil) by means of the blood of the Lamb and by the utterance of their testimony.

I have been able to share this testimony at my church as I placed the prescription bottle on the altar. Giving God the glory in my healing ministered to others in the congregation who were diagnosed with incurable diseases, and currently taking Prednisone or knew of someone who was. God is not a respecter of persons, and since He was able to heal me He can heal others of any sickness, malady, or disease. The Bible says, the Lord heals [each one of] all your diseases (Psalm 103:3, AMP). This has also been a way to share my faith, recite my testimony, pray and lay hands on the sick. My testimony has been a tool to witness to others in the marketplace to lead them to our Great Physician. For when you endure and overcome, you gain experience and then are able to teach others. People can always learn from and be encouraged by someone who has been where they are stationed or going. I encourage others to share and give testimony to what God is doing or has done in your life. You never know the impact you may have on someone's life for healing, deliverance, and breakthrough. I praise God for it now being eleven years that I've been medication-free. I'm a strong believer in natural holistic remedies. Since God created us as living beings from the dust (minerals) of the earth it makes sense to me that it would take living whole foods and minerals, along with fitness, to maintain our health.

Healing the sick is God's will. Jesus says, For I have come down from heaven, not to do My own will, but to do the will of Him who sent Me (John 6:38, AMP).

He personally bore our sins in His [own] body on the tree [as on an altar and offered Himself on it], that we might die (cease to exist) to sin and live to righteousness. By His wounds you have been healed (I Peter 2:24, AMP).

The afflictions in our bodies were laid upon Jesus, and he bore them. Recognize that we do not need to carry or bear them. This is a statement of fact that by Jesus' stripes, we have been healed. This is not something that is going to happen to us but has already happened. We just need to accept that we have already received in faith---by Jesus' stripes, we are already healed.

Strong faith looks at God and nothing or no one else in the midst of adversity. It doesn't take note of the pain, symptoms, the doctor's diagnosis or prognosis. Do not put your faith in the natural realm. Yes we can be thankful and appreciative for those who are in the medical profession. Yet, doctors do not have the final say about the outcome of our lives. God has the final say on when we will take our last breath. It's not about what you see or feel in the natural realm. It's all about what God says. The Bible reads, God who gives life to the dead and calls into being that which does not exist (Romans 4:17, AMP). We have to know what God says. We have to believe what God says. We have to speak what God says back to Him. The doctor told me that I would be on medications for the rest of my life. I boldly chose to get into agreement with what God says. "By His stripes I am healed." "The Lord heals me of all my diseases." "Many are the afflictions of the righteous but the Lord delivers me out of them all." "I shall not die, but live, so that I can declare the works of the Lord." The more you say it, where it gets saturated in your spirit, the more you will believe the Word. Refuse to be passive about your faith. But without faith it is impossible to [walk with God and] please Him, for whoever comes [near] to God must [necessarily] believe that God exists and that He rewards those who [earnestly and diligently] seek Him, (Hebrews 11:6, AMP).

Be encouraged to keep on praying, keep on fasting, keep on speaking the Word, and keep on praising with your eyes fixed on the Lord. He is with us and will never leave us, and we need to take courage to stand on God's Word. Believe the Word of God. Having done all continue to stand, fight your enemy, and win victoriously!

PRAYER OF AFFIRMATION: I thank God for the power of prayer and fasting to break the power of every kind of sickness and disease in my life. I bind the works of the enemy and any attack over my life. I command every spirit of affliction, disease, and disorder to come out of my body. I command every electrical, magnetic, and chemical frequency to align itself in my body to work in proper order. I command all of the good cells in my body to overpower and digest all of the bad cells in my body, in Jesus name. I thank you and praise you for my healing Lord. I thank you that by your stripes I am already healed. I thank you as a believer that I shall lay hands on the sick and they shall recover. I expect the supernatural. (Jeremiah 17:14, I Peter 2:24, St. Mark 16:17-18)

About the Author, Lauretha Ward

Phone: (313)409-0772
Website: www.mindshapeup.com
Facebook: Lauretha Ward
https://www.facebook.com/mindshapeup
Twitter: @LaurethaWard
Instagram: laurethaward https://www.instagram.com/laurethaward
Pinterest: laurethaw https://www.pinterest.com/laurethaw

Lauretha is a professional writer, public speaker, and small business owner currently serving as CEO of Mind Shape Up LLC. She says, "Writing sermon summaries, blogs, and manuscripts is my passion and fulfills part of my purpose in life."

Having battled with suicidal thoughts, an emotional rollercoaster of weight gain and loss, experiencing healing from an incurable disease, and breakthrough from the generational curse of incest, Lauretha

Ward, author, intercessor, and motivational speaker, acknowledges that her "wilderness" experiences of suffering did not allow her to continue to stay in the desert storms of life. Through every trial and pain she drew strength and had a personal breakthrough from prayer and fasting.

Her message via a writing ministry is to offer hope to those who are struggling with challenges in certain areas of everyday life (personal) relationships, financial woes, health issues, and workplace crisis. She will encourage, empower, and positively impact her audience during the tough times, to know that they can make it and their life can be transformed through having their mind daily renewed by His word. She says, "It is about learning to find hope during defeat instead of giving into the negative chatter we all battle with in the mind. Through my personal experiences I can share the tools that I used to be an overcomer and encourage others with how to have victory during the tough times."

Book Lauretha for a speaking engagement at your next event! Laurethaward777@gmail.com.

Stay Connected

Suzanne Doyle-Ingram: www.prominencepublishing.com

Alexandra Romann: www.alexandraromann.com

Alicia Hill-Marceau: http://peaches150.wordpress.com

Dr. Suzanne Sykurski: www.alpinenaturopathic.com

Colleen Preston: www.oasistraining.ca

Holly Henbest: www.henbest.com

Michele Devlin: www.macdevfinancial.com

Rhona Parsons: www.bodyworksbms.com

Rosa Livingstone: www.aloadoffyourmind.com

Jen Hickle: www.neveraloneservices.com

Rochelle Okoye: www.tristarvancouver.com

Lauretha Ward: www.mindshapeup.com

Marsha Vanwynsberghe: www.marshavanw.com

Carrie Ware: www.carrieware.ca

Sheri Scott: www.SpringhouseArchitects.com

Would YOU Like to be in our Next Book?

We are looking for contributors to our next book, Shine Volume III.

Do you have a story that you'd like to share? Are you interested in inspiring others? If so, we want you!

Even if you don't feel like a "writer", don't worry. We offer guidance on how to write your chapter and we support you throughout the entire process.

Please contact the Publisher, Suzanne Doyle-Ingram, at www.ProminencePublishing.com for more information.

www.ingramcontent.com/pod-product-compliance
Lightning Source LLC
Chambersburg PA
CBHW060555200326
41521CB00007B/576